Retirement Secrets of Mexico

Russell Blake

Books@RussellBlake.com

ISBN: 979-8-6840595-5-1

Published by

Reprobatio Limited

Accolades for Retirement Secrets of Mexico

As a person who's lived on two continents and four countries, and winged it along the way with often disastrous consequences, I only wish I'd had had a gem of a book like this to guide me before buying a house and moving to a foreign land. You'll find everything here you need to know, plus a few top secrets, especially regarding locations. Written in a fun, intelligent, witty style, and above all, brimming with insider information you won't find anywhere else, if you're thinking, or even just dreaming, of living in Mexico, Blake's book is a must-read essential. Everything from budgets to safety to health care to banking to immigration forms to starting a business to veterinarians, and more, is covered, and within its pages you'll find a smorgasbord of information unlike anything I've seen.

Don't leave home without devouring this book first! After reading Retirement Secrets of Mexico I'm ready to pack my bags and move there! Five glowing stars!

•*USA TODAY* bestselling author, Arianne Richmonde

Worth every peso. Blake strips away the fiction from the facts about relocating to Mexico in detailed, actionable steps. He pulls back the blinds on some of the best hidden gem locations for expats in Mexico, as well as exposes truth about the beautiful culture and lifestyle Mexico has to offer.

If you've ever considered relocating to Mexico and thought it was too complicated or weren't sure how to get started, this book is your roadmap. So, pour yourself a margarita and dive in.

•*USA TODAY* bestselling author, Ernie Dempsey

From the visionary mind of New York Times Bestselling author Russell Blake comes a must-read guide on expatriation to paradise—without the tequila hangover. Blake serves up shot after shot of no-nonsense tactics, tips, and considerations on how to make Viva Mexico your new reality.

Although it's not a sales brochure for Mexico…I'll confess I might have already checked my passport status and combed over real estate listings. When the real world is stranger than fiction, Blake delivers an uppercut of much needed common sense to anyone looking to safeguard and increase his or her quality of life and measure of happiness.

•Amazon #1 Bestselling author of the Nate Temple Series, Shayne Silvers

Author's Note

Before beginning the journey to what will hopefully be an enlightening exploration of the best kept retirement/expatriation secrets south of the border, it seems fitting to introduce myself. My name's Russell Blake, and I'm a NY Times, USA Today, and Wall Street Journal bestselling author of over sixty fiction novels, as well as a serial entrepreneur and custom home designer and builder, who's been living full time in Mexico for 16 years.

My story began when I sold my company in the U.S. and decided to move abroad to see how I liked living outside what I fondly refer to as "the old country." I originally considered Australia and Europe, having spent a lot of time in both places, but opted to give Mexico a try, for what I figured might be six months. I chose it because I was familiar with it from long weekends in Ensenada and Cabo San Lucas and the usual vacation spots on the Pacific coast and in Quintana Roo, and I figured it would be a relatively painless way to dip my toe in the water, so to speak, and get used to being an expat. I also wanted to stay close to the U.S. in case I got homesick or wanted to visit or things didn't work out, and being a couple hours away by plane was an important consideration.

My first stop was Cabo San Lucas, in Baja, where I wound up spending over a decade. From there I branched out, and in my travels around the country serendipitously discovered a suburb of Guadalajara that was unlike anything I thought existed in Mexico. I became so enamored of the area that I decided to move and spend a lot of my time there, enjoying a European, cosmopolitan lifestyle in a neighborhood that would give Beverly Hills a run for its money. I wound up building a second home and split my time between the beach in Cabo and the city in Guadalajara. From there I further discovered a number of other relatively unknown spots that are perfect candidates for Americans or Canadians (hereafter "Gringos" in the book) to spend their lives in comfort, safety, and enjoying an unbelievably opulent lifestyle on a fraction of the cost of their home country – in some of which I have invested or started businesses.

I grew up in California and New York, and as an adult traveled extensively throughout the U.S. and Europe, so I'm accustomed to "first world" environments and facilities. And while I celebrate diversity of different cultures, I still expect certain levels of comfort and reliability and availability of consumer goods, as well as modern health care and security. I'll confess a weakness for fine dining and good wine, as well as a taste for nice cars, beautiful architecture, and the better things in life. While I could write a tome about how to live on a pauper's income in third world conditions, that's not what this book is about – this book isn't "how to make it on $800 a month in rudimentary conditions." Rather, it's to share some remarkable locations that most Gringos have no idea exist, and offer my thoughts on them; places where your dollar goes further by a mile, where home prices and rents harken back to the 1980's, and where if you know what you're doing, you can live a platinum lifestyle on a *cerveza* budget. In other words, this isn't intended to be a guide to the very cheapest places you can live in Mexico, but rather, the very best value places where you can live extremely well, in safety, comfort, with good health care, great restaurants, and reasonable infrastructure.

Big promises, I know. But I've done it for coming up on two decades, and in my journey have found places that are truly secret to most, including the lion's share of Mexicans – which came as a surprise at first. I mean, I figured that Mexicans must know all the best spots in their own country, but that's not true. Mexico is a big place, and like the U.S., most are only familiar with where they live, and maybe where they vacation. Most of the locales I'm going to share with you are neither vacation hotspots, nor are they accessible to most Mexicans – because the very best places don't have much in the way of industry, which is a must for the aspirational or the upwardly mobile looking to work their way up the income and societal ladder. But that very same characteristic makes them amazing places for those who have a retirement or social security income. And I have to tell you, after having started or been instrumental in over a half dozen businesses since moving abroad, even those locales have surprising opportunity for those of an entrepreneurial bent who can think outside the box.

I don't want to get ahead of myself, but I'll outline the characteristics I value so you have an idea of my tastes, and the rough structure of this book so you understand how the information is organized.

I will spotlight eight areas I believe are among the best in Mexico. They have low crime, warm weather, are affordable, feature quality health care, good restaurants, quality amenities, and are places I'd be more than happy to hang my hat for long stretches. I'll feature a moderate size town with platinum level golf course living that has it all as far as I'm concerned; an unknown suburb of a major city with a vibrant culture and extraordinary cuisine, nightlife, and amenities; a metro area that's about as laid back as they come with shoestring costs; a lakeside expat hideaway a stone's throw from a major international airport; a bustling colonial city that features the best of old world charm, and several jewels of Baja that are far more than the rowdy cantina towns most are familiar with.

I'll cover everything you need to know to evaluate them. Costs, documentation required, banking, schools, health care, crime and safety, expat groups, weather, shopping, home ownership and renting, pets, and everything else that comes up when folks ask me what they need to understand about the places in order to feel at home.

By the time you finish reading, you should have a clear idea of each locale, and what they offer, as well as any negatives. This book isn't a whitewashing of any spot, and doesn't sugarcoat the downsides. There's no place on earth that doesn't have negatives, and one of my problems with many of the books I've read that purport to be guides like this is they wax positive about the upsides, and omit or skim over the downsides. I don't do that, because you're paying to learn the truth, not some idealized version of it.

I chose a variety of places, because budgets and desired lifestyles will vary. With the exception of Cabo, I've deliberately avoided the more popular tourist destinations, like Puerto Vallarta, Mazatlan, Acapulco, Cancun, Tulum, Playa Del Carmen – mainly because there are significant safety concerns because of crime that make them unsuitable for my endorsement, or there are few if any bargains to be found, or because the weather is unbearable for long stretches of the year, and because they're overrun with Gringos already so there's no need for a book pretending they're secrets. They aren't, they're widely publicized, and I find many of them have all the charm of any other tourist destination where you're the prey for the local predators. I also avoid towns like San Miguel de Allende, Oaxaca, and Ensenada that are relatively high profile to Americans. We're talking relative secrets, not towns that see large numbers of Gringos every year and are on the map in every way due to regular features in major American newspapers.

And please. If I don't touch on your favorite place, it isn't because I dislike it. It's that I only have so many pages, and I don't like to feature spots I know too little about or that I feel are dangerous or overpriced or lack the type of infrastructure I value. While it's certainly possible to find unlimited charm in areas that are relatively primitive by US standards, that isn't the point of this book. I want a modern hospital, good food handling, reasonable roads, availability of creature comforts, fast internet, affordable housing built to decent standards…not a lifestyle where I'm hanging with chickens and the nearest grocery store is a half hour drive down a poorly maintained track. If that's your thing, you may find some nuggets here, but the thrust of the book is on places that won't feel too alien or require years of adjustment to fit in.

So whether your dream is living large as a couple on your social security, or on $50K and up in a trendy hotspot, you'll find some standout ideas that you probably had no idea existed. In each case I was shocked to discover them, and I own property and investments in most of them, so I put my money where my mouth is.

Taking that first step to a new life isn't easy, and it can be scary for many. The purpose of this book is to make it less so. By the time you turn the last page, hopefully you'll have a good feel for what you're considering getting into, and will be able to book tickets to visit your choices with confidence – or you'll have decided that maybe the whole thing isn't really for you, and you'd be better served looking elsewhere.

But whether you're after a vacation home to spend half a year, or a full-time lifestyle away from the madding crowds, I hope to open your eyes to some new ideas, and to share my enthusiasm for a lifestyle I wouldn't trade for any amount of money.

With that, let's get down to business and look at what I consider to be the finds of a lifetime.

Contents

Chapter 1

–

Introduction

Mexico.

Sunny skies, blue water, balmy nights, icy *cerveza,* a simple and slower pace with a lack of complications or demands. For decades, wealthy Hollywood celebrities in the know came for the incredible fishing and the stunning natural beauty of Baja and Pacific coast resort towns.

It's natural that those north of the border look south with longing, as well as some justified trepidation. For all its incredible diversity and friendly natives, it's unfamiliar as well – a different language, different money, different laws, different customs. And the average American has been propagandized into believing it's a dangerous hell hole where you're taking your life in your hands by walking down the street. As a longtime periodic visitor to the area, I can appreciate the pull of the region, as well as the trepidation that is a natural part of considering cutting the cord and moving to a different country.

When I took the plunge sixteen years ago there were virtually no guides that really helped me with the minutiae of doing so. That's still the case today. There are some well-intentioned periodicals that contain cursory articles in between the advertisements, and some decent on-line publications that try their best to be helpful, but nothing that truly prepares one for the reality of crossing the border and beginning a new life in Mexico.

This book is intended to offer a roadmap and a nuts and bolts guide to choosing a locale and moving. As virtually every aspect of American life has grown increasingly difficult, it's no surprise more people want out. Crime, ruinous taxation, arbitrary application of the rule of law, double standards, destruction of privacy and freedoms, skyrocketing costs, a financial and political system in disarray…it's no wonder many are looking across the border and thinking, "I want my place in the sun while I still have a few good summers left."

The good news is I'm living proof you can make the change, and not only survive, but prosper. I can't tell you the number of times I've said to friends and family, "If I'd known thirty years ago what I know now, I would have bailed and had a far better life for my effort." And that's no lie or exaggeration.

Things are better here. Not everything – some are markedly inferior. But overall, life is better. Just in general. I think a big reason that things seem that way is because the U.S. are consumer-driven societies, where citizens are on a treadmill that increases in speed incrementally over time, until one day they wake up and are in a flat-out run just to stay even. I see it reflected in the driving habits, where motorists are on each others' bumpers at sixty miles per hour, cutting each other off, hyper-reactive and over-stimulated. I see it in the overall impatience people demonstrate in a line or whenever they have to wait. I see it in the constant drive to buy more crap in order to feel good, or to keep up with the Joneses. In the anger and frustration simmering just beneath the surface. In the "all's fair" and dog eat dog approach to business. To my eye it's unhealthy, and it creates tremendous stress and pressure.

Having come from that environment, I can tell you once you've been in Mexico for a while, you'll look at your neighbors to the North as though they're crazy. Because in a lot of ways they are. And it will amuse you no end when you have friends come to visit, and they tell you they think you're very brave, or are unhinged, by wanting to get out of the system and move to a foreign land. You'll look at them with the new awareness that all the fears and uncertainty about making the move are illusory, and that if they only knew how improved their life could be south of the border, they too would be scrambling to figure out a way to get the hell out.

This book's purpose is to tell you what it's like to do so, and give you guidance on how to do it, as well as how to choose where you want to end up living. If you're reading this, you're likely smart enough to understand things aren't going in a positive direction where you are, and you want to make your break while it's still practical to do so. Join the club. There are a lot of you arriving at the same conclusion around the same time in history, and the good news is that it's not only an achievable goal to depart and find a better place to live out your life, but it's not all that hard with some preparation and realistic expectations.

By the time you finish reading *Retirement Secrets of Mexico,* you'll know what you're doing. Congratulations. All journeys begin with the first step, and taking the time to read this puts you miles ahead of those who are doing nothing to achieve their dreams; who are merely existing instead of looking to live better. You'll be convinced by the final chapters you have the ability and the counsel to make the move, and if your experience is anything like mine, you'll find it's the best thing you ever did in your life.

~ ~ ~

When you get across the border, the air smells and feels different. Exotic. Richer. More real. It's as though you've gone from the artificial to the genuine, from the sterility of the synthetic to the organic of the natural.

Mexico has its own feel to it, a feel unlike anywhere else on earth, and the more time you spend in its various attractions, the more you'll grow to appreciate its uniqueness. It's not just because of the hum of activity in Spanish, or the unfamiliar jumble of the town streets typical of the region's lackadaisical approach to central planning, or the aroma of spices from the corner *taquerias*. It's that everything really is different, and yet not so different you feel displaced or lost.

That sense of the exotic blended with the familiar is a function of the large impact Gringos have had on Mexico. We've been going to Mexico for fifty years or so, and much of the prosperity in the larger communities is directly linked to tourism. As the world economy has grown more homogenous and globalized, so too has Mexico, and in many ways it's difficult to tell a mid-sized Mexican city apart from one in other areas of the world, even the U.S.

The purpose of this guide is to provide you with enough

information to be dangerous when evaluating an area to live in Mexico, and to offer enough guidance so most of your questions are answered in the following pages. It isn't a cheerleading manual or an advertisement, and it doesn't seek to convince you Mexico is the dream destination of the western world, where brothers and sisters of all races and creeds dance together in utopian streets. Instead, it attempts to provide you with a balanced description of the place, with the positives and negatives plainly articulated, so you can figure out if it's a good fit for you.

I'll say up front I wouldn't want to live anywhere else other than Mexico, and I've lived in a lot of places. Europe, Canada, all over the U.S., with extended stays in Australia, Hawaii, and Central and South America. So I'm clearly biased, however biased with the knowledge and understanding that comes from having lived in a lot of different cultures and places.

Depending on what you favor, you can find it all in Mexico at a fraction of the cost north of the border, whether it's a cantina town on a forgotten beach or a more European feel, with sidewalk cafes and bohemian charm and a sense of old-world culture.

As we go through the chapters, I hope to offer some insights as to the differences in the various areas. Once you get a feel for those distinctions, if you're really serious about moving, I'd propose you hop on a plane and visit several of the areas that sound the most appealing for your lifestyle.

What this book is not intended to be is a travel guide for Mexico, nor an in-depth description of every major metropolitan area. I will cover the areas I prefer, namely Todos Santos, San Jose Del Cabo, and Cabo San Lucas, Colima, Guadalajara, Merida, Queretaro, and Lake Chapala. Note I've excluded anything within fifty miles of the border – I do so due to the heightened crime and safety concerns in those areas, which are legitimate and not to be taken lightly.

The book is organized in a fairly linear manner, and deals with the most common issues one encounters when considering the move. First is obviously the question of where in Mexico is right for you; followed by logistical topics like taxes and visas, property ownership, banking and money, health care, crime and safety issues, and a host of other mundanities involved in making the trip south for good.

The chapters deliver an unvarnished take on the pros and the cons of living here. I'm assuming if you're reading this it's because you're either evaluating whether moving to Mexico makes sense for you, or you've decided to move, and want a blow-by-blow description of the things you need to know to do so with a minimum of drama.

If you're evaluating whether Mexico is a good fit, I'll offer some observations about life here, and throw out some questions for you to consider before you make any decisions. Let's start off with, what are you expecting when you move to Mexico? Before proceeding any further, think about that for a while, and then get out a piece of paper and on the left-hand side jot down what the attractions for you are – the benefits and the high points. Make a column from top to bottom, and draw a line down the middle of the page. If you're like me, you'll have things like weather, or freedom, or cheaper living listed on the left. Then, on the right side, list all the things that are question marks or concerns, or open issues that might keep you from moving. Again, if you're like me, that column might contain items like safety, or health care, or distance from relatives, or language.

When you consider your list in the context of this book, the goal is to answer any questions or concerns you have on the right side of the page, and do a reality check on the perceived positives on the left side of the page. By the time we're done you should feel confident your list is complete and any concerns have been addressed. If your reasoning process works like mine, you'll be left with a long list of strong positives confirmed to be correct and accurate, and a realistic list of negatives or items that are different than you thought. On balance, the positives should wildly outweigh the negatives, leaving you inspired and confident in your choice to make Mexico your home.

The Merits of Escape

There are scores of reasons for wanting to leave the U.S., most of them by now abundantly clear to even the most patriotic stalwarts. There's the ever-growing, invasive role of government in virtually every aspect of life. There's the steady erosion of civil liberties. There's the 2008 economic crisis and its aftermath, and the lessons it taught – that the banks and pecuniary interests on Wall Street have one set of rules, whereas we all have another, and the taxpayers bail them out whenever they get one wrong; which has been reprised in 2020 with the COVID "emergency economic measures" that are largely handouts to the corporate and financial class at the direct expense of the population.

There's the legitimate concern over the gazillion taxes that have been imposed upon the citizenry over the last hundred years. There's the worry over Social Security, and whether it will even be around twenty years from now, or if so, will buy more than dog food. There's concern over a declining standard of living for the majority, civil unrest, racial turbulence, a growing opioid epidemic, and international policies that are in conflict with our self-image of being the good guys. There's concern over never-ending wars with spiraling costs. There's real question about the stability of the currency, and what it will buy over the next decades.

Many disagree with an income tax policy that seems predatory and unfair, and which confiscates a good amount of your income every year. Some question whether it's a good deal to have to work more than half a year for the state and federal government, and another couple of months to cover the remaining property, sales, gas, liquor, vehicle, cigarette, employment, Social Security, airline, disability, and countless other taxes that have been layered upon the populace over time. As an example, you wind up with maybe thirty percent of your buying power if you live in California after you tally up the impact of Fed, State, and all the rest of these over and hidden taxes. Put bluntly, you're working for the "man" until about the end of September every year, at which point you switch to working for the mortgage company, the credit card companies, and the car companies, until you've covered their interest for the year. And don't forget the accountants who ensure you don't screw up in your calculation of how little you get to keep.

It's no wonder many feel oppressed by the system as it stands – it's been observed that today's working poor and middle class are largely serfs toiling on behalf of the financial/industrial complex, who spend their entire lives toiling on the U.S. plantation trying to save enough to have a comfortable final few years, only to see their shot at it wiped out by one financial swindle and calamity or another.

Many feel they require government permission to do even the most basic and reasonable things, and that increase in the government's role as "Parent" has clamped down and squashed many of their most basic freedoms. Everything requires some department be paid so you can be allowed to do what you don't need permission to do in most of the rest of the world. I've heard it said that U.S. citizens are regarded and treated more like subjects than free men by a government system increasingly intent upon controlling even the most fundamental actions of its population. That's tough to disagree with, especially when viewed from a country where few things require permission.

Believe it or not, one of the things you hear all the time from new arrivals when you live in Mexico is how "free" it feels. That freedom plays a role in a lot of folks' decision-making on choosing Mexico as their new home. But there are countless other reasons for considering the move.

Some just want to go to a place where nobody will bug them if they aren't doing anything to hurt others. Others still want to find a place where their dollar will go a lot further than it will back home. Still others just want a simple life, where the days are spent fishing or chatting with friends over margaritas or tending to a garden, and the nights are warm and filled with mariachis and delicious food.

Whatever your reasons, there's a lot to be said for departing the land of the free and home of the brave and moving to a land where nobody is particularly intent upon getting involved in your affairs or bothering you much.

Now, an important caveat when it comes to the money and tax issue. As a U.S. citizen, you're required to still pay Federal income tax even if you live outside the country. There is a foreign earned income exclusion that's pretty generous ($107+K per year per person) if you earn a living outside the U.S., however for the purposes of this section I'll assume you aren't generating any Mexican income. Either way, you're still required to file. Having said that, I know many folks living in Mexico who've decided not to bother, and don't seem much worse for the experience. That's risky to do given Mexican banking laws unless you have another citizenship (if you're a U.S. citizen), however if you work on a strictly cash basis and have no assets in the U.S., it can be done.

I'm not handing out financial advice, nor would I even suggest you break any laws, however I can observe that if you don't have property in the U.S. and only have a bank account with a minimum amount of money there, reality is there isn't a whole lot to attach should you get into a disagreement with the government. I'm going to stay away from extending any advice on how you should structure your personal affairs, other than saying that you need to be comfortable with whatever you decide to do. Whatever your thinking, consult a qualified tax advisor before making any decisions.

Some decide to cut the cord completely and disappear, also for a host of reasons. I've met people ducking abusive spouses, bill collectors, the taxman, a life they never felt gave them what they wanted. I've encountered plenty of men who looked South to find a mate with traditional values. I've met entrepreneurs who came to Mexico because they couldn't start or operate businesses in the U.S. due to burdens of regulation and taxes and minimum costs. I've met people with dual or triple citizenships (legal, by the way, for U.S. citizens) who one day decided they didn't need their American passport anymore. I've met scoundrels and flim-flam men trying to evade their victims or the long arm of the law. But I've mostly met normal people who just had it with their way of life, and decided to chuck it all and look to more hospitable climes. Some were just sick of cold weather. Some just decided to try it for a few months, and stayed for decades.

Deciding to leave your home country is a big step, and it can be either frightening, or energizing, depending upon your circumstances and how you frame your perception (and what's motivating the move). A lot of it is mental. If you spend much time dwelling on all the things you'll be giving up, and how different things are in a negative (versus positive) way, or view a move as a step down in quality, you're going to be pretty unhappy. If you view it as a release from the old and an opportunity for reinvention, a bold step in the direction of improvement of quality of life and an abandonment of the constraints and conventions that have brought little or no enjoyment to your existence, a second chance to do or be whatever you really want to be...well, I think you can see how perspective can make a huge difference.

Again, I've met all kinds in my travels here, but the ones who seem to do best are the folks who embrace the new, and celebrate the differences in cultures rather than stew over them. One gentleman in particular comes to mind – he's eighty-four years old, and I met him over an icy *cerveza* one evening at a local hangout in Cabo San Lucas. He was dancing with the two comely waitresses, and having a hell of a time. That got my curiosity going, and I asked him how long he'd been here and what had brought him to the area. He told me he'd been a fisherman in Washington and later Alaska, and had come here twenty years ago with his wife when they'd retired because he'd been tired of the cold and the rain. His wife had passed away a decade ago of natural causes, and he'd been occupying his time by fishing on the beach every day, doing a two hour hike every morning, playing with his dogs, spending time with his countless friends in the area, and hanging out a few nights a week and kicking his heels up. He indicated he hates old people, and whenever he gets old he plans to just lie down and die. Thinks that may happen in another twenty years or so. Meanwhile, it's Pacifico and dancing with the waitresses for him.

The one thing I can tell you as you consider moving to Mexico is that attitude is everything. You can be miserable anywhere, and you can be happy anywhere, depending on your perspective. The one trait that everyone who's done well in Mexico possesses is that they feel like they're missing exactly nothing by living there. I share that perspective, and it's a common one among the expats. The ones that don't do so well constantly harp on "the old country" and how much more modern or convenient some things are. Those are the ones who manage to be unhappy in paradise. If you're reading this, you likely aren't in that club.

Regardless of motivation, escape can be refreshing and invigorating, a new beginning for whatever reasons drive you. How you handle your personal journey is a matter of choice, and the following chapters are designed to help you get acclimated and navigate the waters like a native.

Why Mexico?

Fair question. Why not Costa Rica, or Guatemala, or Belize? Or Chile, Argentina, Ecuador, El Salvador, Panama?

First and foremost is because much of Mexico is proximate enough to the U.S., and has enough of a connection with it in terms of tourists and vacation home owners and expats, that the areas I will describe more closely resembles the U.S. in terms of creature comforts then many of the aforementioned places. They're a few hours by plane from most of the western U.S., which is shorter than some people's commutes to work. So if there's a major medical emergency, you can be in the U.S. in a couple hours. Also, if you have relatives or friends who want to visit, or if you want to go back to the States for any reason, it's a short hop. That's reassuring to many new expats, as the psychology of being so close, but yet so far, has appeal, at least for the first months of expatriation.

Second is the weather. Most of Mexico is sunny and warm almost year-round, and depending on the area could have only a few days of rain each year, or a Hawaii style rainy season where it comes down a few hours in the evenings and is clear the rest of the day. That creates a very real "endless summer" feel to many of the locales I'll cover, and especially Baja, which was a huge draw for me when I moved here. If you want five or six months a year of rain go to Costa Rica or Panama. Ditto if your thing is malaria.

Another big draw is the language. While the official language is Spanish, most of the metro areas have large populations of English speakers. The reason is obvious – for years, all tourists came from America, thus if you wanted to make more money in any endeavor it helped if you were relatively fluent in English. So there isn't a huge obstacle in terms of the language, at least for the everyday tasks, in most of the areas I'll speak to. And English is now taught in most schools, so any of the younger generation will usually understand you, if not be able to converse. That said, the bureaucracy largely doesn't speak English (or pretends not to – after all, you're in Mexico, so why would you expect Mexican bureaucrats to speak your language?), however that gap has been filled with numerous entrepreneurs who will assist you with any task requiring *Español.*

I came speaking very little Spanish other than what I'd picked up ordering margaritas and asking for the bill at restaurants, and encountered virtually no difficulty in ninety-nine percent of my interactions. There are folks who have lived here full time for decades who speak maybe ten words. Over the years, I've made an effort to learn the language, as it seems lazy and arrogant to live someplace and not even try to acclimate, and I can honestly say I'm now adept at conversational Spanish. MP3 courses helped, as did getting a Mexican girlfriend. Especially the girlfriend. One learns what one needs to, and focuses one's attentions where they're required. But you don't need to hook up with one of the locals to learn the lingo – just being immersed in it will get you started, and as you make friends, you'll naturally pick up more as you go along.

A big attraction is also the pace and the culture. Things are relaxed in many areas, very much like on most tropical islands. In Baja or Chapala you're dressed for dinner or a meeting if you have on shorts and a T-shirt, and in most other places jeans and a polo shirt are all you'll need. There are few places or occasions where you really need to do much but roll out of bed to be ready for anything. That's a strong positive if you've spent decades donning suits or uniforms. And the dress code is a good indicator of the level of formality. Things are extremely *laisser faire*, and the locals don't really have much interest in bothering you if you aren't going out of your way to bother them.

While there are laws and rules, common sense tends to dominate daily events rather than the letter of the law. While the culture is overwhelmingly Catholic, at least officially, Mexico is a place where there isn't a lot of judging going on. The philosophy can best be described as, "You're an adult, whatever you want to do, knock yourself out, just don't hurt anybody."

That lack of judgment by others extends across the gamut of behaviors and habits. Mexico certainly has its share of Gringos who chucked it all one day, pointed the car south, and spent the next decade wasting away in Margaritaville. It's easy to do, as nobody particularly sees anything wrong with sitting on the beach at ten AM with a cold beer, or being out at a nightclub at three AM, so the culture is very accepting of virtually everything.

One exception is drugs. Officially, drugs are bad, and the laws are extremely severe for use or possession – although recently possession of small amounts of drugs for personal use were decriminalized. Unofficially, Marijuana is ubiquitous, and most substances can be had easily and cheaply. I don't do drugs, so that's not my thing, but my feeling is that if you want to smoke a joint instead of having a beer to soften life's blows, knock yourself out. Here, as with all things, my counsel is to use your head. If you make yourself a target and flout the law, you can expect problems at some point. If you're discreet about whatever it is you're doing, you can probably expect nobody to pay any attention. One important caveat: if your expatriation plan involves selling drugs or trafficking them in Mexico, you should also take out a large life insurance policy naming me as the beneficiary, as you'll likely wind up in about thirty pieces in a garbage bag somewhere in the desert, or rotting in a cell that makes Calcutta look like the Ritz for the rest of your short life.

Speaking of drugs, most everything you need a prescription for in the U.S. you don't here. That translates into most drugs costing a fraction of their price in the U.S., which is a big benefit to most retirees who have some condition or the other requiring pills to be popped. There are pharmacies on virtually every corner, and the only thing you'll need prescriptions for are antibiotics (due to concerns over drug-resistant strains of bacteria) and controlled substances like Xanax, Valium or Vicadin. And you can thank the U.S. for that, as it's because of concessions for American anti-drug money poured into Mexico (to no effect I can detect) that even those tranquilizers or pain killers aren't available without prescription. I'll go into all this in more detail in the chapter on health care, however the take-away at this point is that you'll be able to get anything you need, within reason, at a fraction of the cost and with little or no hassles.

And while we're on the topic of cost, I would be remiss if I didn't mention probably the number one reason for expats to move to Mexico and wind up staying: price. Basically, whatever your flavor or budget, you can find it here. If your plan is to live on $1500 (all dollar amounts in this guide are U.S. dollars) a month as a couple, you can do it in some of the areas I'll cover, but it won't be the same as if you have $3000. Depending upon where you decide to live and what your lifestyle requires, a high quality of life can be had at virtually any price point. It's true that the high-profile tourist areas like Cabo can cost as much to live in as San Diego, but it's also true that you can live even there with a pretty nice situation for a few grand a month. It all depends upon what you're looking for. On average, Mexico is about 60-70% cheaper than the U.S., with the exception of Baja, because everything has to be shipped over or trucked down 1000 miles of highway. If real budget living is your goal, you'd be best served skipping Cabo and Guadalajara, and look to Colima or Merida – areas where a retired couple can live extremely well for $2K or so a month.

There is an important dynamic that keep Mexico affordable, and it's the salaries – the average local makes $300 to $600 a month, maybe more, maybe less. In some areas it might be half that. But still, the income levels are such that the local economies can't command high prices for the locals – only the tourists, and generally only in the most obviously touristy areas. So if in Cabo San Lucas, to choose the most expensive of the places I'll cover in this book, stay away from the waterfront restaurants demanding $50 for a steak, and instead venture inland 3 blocks and get the same steak for $15 or less. As an example, I recently had chicken Mole at a touristy restaurant replete with colorful art, watery margaritas, and polished mariachis, for $22 – for a chicken breast with some Mole sauce on it, and a scoop of rice. Several days later I had the same dish in a place two blocks off the beaten path, but still proximate to the action, and paid $5. And the margaritas, which were stronger and tastier, cost $3.50 instead of $14.

The lower wages also mean you can afford little luxuries you might have never considered back home. You can have a massage for around $10-$20 anywhere in Mexico. You can get a good haircut for $5 or so. Ditto for manicures. A maid will run you $300 or so a month full time, or $15 for four hours, once a week. You can quickly see how quality of life can increase even as cost-to-live drops sharply. Quite simply, labor is so inexpensive that you can have the service comforts of a king for much less than it costs you to just live "normally" back home.

And there's the culture, which doesn't really celebrate the material in the same manner as the U.S. Here, if your car is ten years old but runs well, it would never occur to you to get another one. The notion of buying a Rolex is almost unheard of. Nobody but the tourists wear $100 shirts or $140 tennis shoes. The entire materialism thing takes a back seat to sensible, sustainable living. Sure, you'll see recent arrivals who just don't get it or the nouveaux riche driving around in Humvees or Benz SUV's, but only in the most prosperous towns. Most prefer brands like Ford or Toyota to Mercedes or BMW, for maintenance reasons, but also because nobody wants to be a target for the cops – if you're dumb enough to drive around in a $70K vehicle in an area where the average cop makes $400 a month, you're hanging a sign around your neck saying, "Stop me, I'll give you money as I have more of it than good sense!"

For the most part, Mexico celebrates understatement and conservative living, and as such your costs recede to only things you really want or need. You aren't inundated with constant bombardments designed to get you to spend, spend, spend, so you lose the desire to do so pretty quickly.

All of this and more will be covered in the following chapters, however the point is that there are many strong positives to escaping to Mexico for good.

Pros and Cons of the Culture

The areas I'll recommend are relaxed – far more so than most places in the U.S. Gone from most undertakings is any sense of pressing urgency. The pace of the culture is one where the inevitable *mañana* attitude of Latin America is taken to a whole new level.

Meals can take several hours, and are important bonding events – this is when groups socialize and spend time together, which is one of the primary goals of Mexican culture. Mexico is a place where even people who don't know you say hello when you enter a store or a restaurant, and where great premium is placed upon being friendly and sociable. This has been described to me as being eerily akin to America in the 1950's, when few locked their doors and most knew their neighbors, as well as most of the members of their community.

People here like to socialize, and they're open to making new friends at the drop of a hat. The culture celebrates friendship and interaction beyond most other virtues, which is a positive if you're looking for a healthier environment in which to live, but is a negative if you're looking to get things done quickly. If it's a choice between doing some task, or stopping and chatting for half an hour with an old (or just met) acquaintance, Mexicans will inevitably choose the more social of the possibilities. It's just the way things are, and should be celebrated.

Malcolm Gladwell wrote a book called "Outliers" in which he describes a community in Pennsylvania where heart disease was half the norm in the U.S., and where cardiovascular problems were unheard of in anyone under fifty-five. In fact, death from all causes was thirty-five percent below the national averages, and yet the population ate tons of fatty foods, drank like fish, and smoked like chimneys. From the introduction of Outliers:

"The results were astonishing. In Roseto, virtually no one under 55 died of a heart attack, or showed any signs of heart disease. For men over 65, the death rate from heart disease in Roseto was roughly half that of the United States as a whole. The death rate from all causes in Roseto, in fact, was something like thirty or thirty-five percent lower than it should have been…

…"There was no suicide, no alcoholism, no drug addiction, and

very little crime. They didn't have anyone on welfare. Then we looked at peptic ulcers. They didn't have any of those either. These people were dying of old age. That's it."

...What Wolf slowly realized was that the secret of Roseto wasn't diet or exercise or genes or the region where Roseto was situated. It had to be the Roseto itself. As Bruhn and Wolf walked around the town, they began to realize why. They looked at how the Rosetans visited each other, stopping to chat with each other in Italian on the street, or cooking for each other in their backyards. They learned about the extended family clans that underlay the town's social structure. They saw how many homes had three generations living under one roof, and how much respect grandparents commanded. They went to Mass at Our Lady of Mt. Carmel Church and saw the unifying and calming effect of the church. They counted twenty-two separate civic organizations in a town of just under 2000 people. They picked up on the particular egalitarian ethos of the town, that discouraged the wealthy from flaunting their success and helped the unsuccessful obscure their failures."

Gladwell is describing a sense of old-world community that had astounding health consequences for the residents of the town of Roseto, PA. This study took place in the 1960's, however the lesson is germane to Baja today; which is quite simply very much like 1960's era Roseto, where the pace and the social structure emphasizes values and a lifestyle that are antipodal to that of modern America.

There's just way less stress and pressure. As described, meals are events that can take hours, and socializing is a priority for most any undertaking. And the *Siesta* is a way of life. All over Mexico, towns close down from two to four PM so that folks can have a relaxed lunch followed by a *Siesta*. To an American, this can at first seem astounding, however I can tell you from personal experience that the *Siesta* is probably one of the most important Mexican innovations aside from tacos and tequila.

The attitude towards the elderly is different than in the U.S. as well, in that there is a general respect for older folks. This isn't a dog-eat-dog culture of hyper-competition, so people are more patient with those at retirement age, and treat them with considerably more courtesy than in the States, where they are often viewed as an annoyance. That's a big boon if you have some gray hair.

Mexico is a low-pressure zone, where the pace is easily half or less that of even the slowest places in the U.S. When a friend says they'll be at dinner at 8PM, it's not considered late if they show up at 8:30 or 8:45. If a clerk says it will be ten minutes before your order will be ready, that could easily mean up to an hour, with no blinking or apology. That's great for your blood pressure, however if you're a "Type A" personality it can drive you nuts.

My advice is to alter your expectations to be in line with those of the region. There's not a lot of point of maintaining an aggressive or punctual nature in a world where that's considered anxious or rude. What will happen is you'll find that within the first six months of living here, most every concern and issue will have miraculously melted away, to be replaced with a sense of wellbeing and contentment that Gringos pay tens of thousands of dollars to therapists and pharmacists to achieve. That's because you'll discover you only fret over the things that matter, versus being an over-stimulated rat in a maze.

As I've observed before, in the U.S., the entire economy is driven by the consumer, and as such, there's a built-in social imperative to keep the population consuming at all costs. What that translates into is a world where consumerism – the constant buying of items you don't need money you don't have – is a national trait. That's why you'll see the government terribly concerned when consumer spending dips. Consumerism is everything, but the only way to get people to buy increasing amounts of junk they neither need nor particularly want is to make them feel miserable much of the time, with the only hope of feeling better residing in buying junk.

It's impossible to get people to trade houses every few years, or get a new car every three, or to buy multiples of everything, unless they believe they'll feel good if they do so. But to keep the machine going, you can't have them feel too good for too long, or they stop buying once they're done. So the high from the attainment of the good or service has to be short-lived, with the only hope of feeling good again to buy something else. It's like Lucy from Peanuts with the ball – Charlie Brown knows her promise to hold the ball is always a lie, but he's compelled to try to kick it anyway; it's his only hope of feeling good, and even if it didn't work the last hundred times, the promise is that *this* time it might just be different and satisfy his need.

That's probably why so much of the American population is on anti-depressants, and most are playing a never-ending game of keep up with the Joneses. They've been indoctrinated since birth with constant ads, articles, programs, and social messages that drive them to buy, buy, buy – even if they lack the money to do so. That's where credit comes in. Spend money you don't have to buy something you either need to feel decent, or that will convince others that you're successful, or whatever the imperative is. It's a guarantee you'll never really feel very good – people who feel good don't particularly care about what everyone else is doing or thinking; that is to say well-adjusted people generally don't buy a lot of unnecessary garbage. And that's bad for business, even if it's good for you as an individual. The culture is one of buy more, all the time. Shopping is celebrated as a form of near-religion in women's magazines, and countless TV programs are devoted to the shopping exploits of celebrities or wannabe celebrities. The messages are constant and consistent: buy, buy, buy.

Mexico is the polar opposite. In Mexico, the vast majority don't have a whole lot of wealth and debt isn't used almost at all, nor do they have the drive or the opportunity to go from rags to any sort of riches, so the societal imperative is more one of satisfaction with what one has, and of prizing relationships and experiences over material possessions. Family matters a great deal, as the family is the safety net for older relatives and those starting new households. Families stick together, and everyone helps out with child care and dealing with the elderly. One of the primary reasons for this is that no real social programs exist to help, so there's no expectation of entitlement of care or assistance. Your family is all you have, so you treat them well in the hopes they'll return the favor.

The same goes for neighbors. Often, when something goes

wrong, the neighbors will be there far before any police or other assistance will, so neighbors tend to know each other and try to help each other. Today's help from you may need to be reciprocated tomorrow by your neighbor, thus everyone tends to be more courteous and friendly than in the States. In Mexico, most everyone living around you will know you, and you them. It creates a much stronger sense of community, driven by a mutual assistance ethic that's cultural.

As another example, you will find that drivers tend to be courteous rather than aggressive and rude. That's because of the culture of politeness, but also because at any point, the guy you just passed and flipped off may wind up passing *you* in twenty minutes, right after your front tire blew out and you're stranded by the side of the road in the heat. In Mexico, you wind up getting a far better sense of how much better life is if you use a bit of honey versus venom and vinegar, versus the U.S., where most have never even met their neighbors and don't want to. People are nicer because they understand they need each other to persevere and thrive, and because many of the towns in Mexico are relatively small, so they understand they'll be seeing each other often.

So strong positives in the culture, quality of life, courtesy and pace departments. All of which have downsides, as well. Things can take forever, even simple things, and you can never expect nor depend on efficient execution. You could order the same dish at the same restaurant three different evenings, and every time it could come out a little different. Things aren't mass produced, thus virtually everything has hand-made idiosyncrasies. Coming from a society where you can get food twenty-four hours a day, spat out with digital regularity from spotlessly clean but lifeless franchises, some areas of Mexico will seem primitive. But it isn't. Not really. It's just different, in a largely good way.

Inefficiency can also translate into challenges, especially with bureaucracy, law enforcement and corruption. As an example, if you get pulled over in Mexico, depending on the area you're likely to get off with a warning after "tipping" the officer a few hundred pesos. Some would argue that's corruption. I tend to agree, but can also think of it as a more efficient delivery system – you sort of pay on the spot for your transgression, and all the rest of the bureaucracy is eliminated from the equation, resulting in a lower cost. I will say that although I've heard stories, I've never been pulled over unfairly down here, and I've never paid even close to what I would have in the States for the same violation on the few occasions I have been pulled over. Doesn't mean it never happens, but just not to me.

Don't get me wrong – I'm not condoning nor approving of dangerous behavior, whether there's a strict penalty or a hand slap. I'm just using it as an example.

Another recurring complaint Gringos have is that the bureaucracy here takes forever to get anything accomplished – which is completely true. *Mañana* is a way of life, so one gets accustomed to it, and instead of fighting it learns to accept it. I know when I go in to Immigration that no matter what I'm told in terms of a wait, to multiply by at least four. That's just the way it is. It's also much the same way in most other places, including much of North America. Think about the lightning-like efficiency of your local DMV, for instance, and you'll get a sense of how all state offices work. You can either prepare yourself for that aspect of the culture and learn to grin and bear it, or you can blow a gasket and get carried out in a body bag. Either way, it will be this way far longer than you'll be around, so my advice is to simply understand that the pace is slower, and deal with it. Again, expectations are key to satisfaction.

No segment on the culture would be complete without mentioning the court system. Things work much slower in Mexico, so anything requiring a judge to resolve it can take many years, or even decades. That's a negative if you've been wronged, but a strong positive in that suing is the last resort in Mexico as conflict resolution, not the first. In the U.S., if you spill hot coffee in your lap, or trip outside a restaurant, or have a disagreement with your neighbor, there's likely an attorney eagerly waiting to take your issue to court. Here it's the opposite, for the most part. If you trip or spill coffee, the attitude is that you might want to be more careful. If you have a dispute with your neighbor, you might want to work at coming up with a resolution everyone can live with rather than expecting justice from the court system. Virtually the only people I know who are involved in lawsuits in Mexico are Gringos suing other Gringos. It's a shame, but I suppose old habits die hard, and we've managed to export that one South with us. The problem is that it really doesn't work, as you'll likely die of old age before anything definitive happens in court.

If you're litigious you're in for a big letdown in Mexico.

Creating Income in Mexico

Let me start off by saying that I don't recommend moving to Mexico with an eye towards getting rich quickly, or even making good money. It can be done, but unlike most "escape" guides that make it sound as easy as falling off a log, I'll be honest and tell you that it's as hard, or harder, to make a livable wage in Mexico as it is anywhere else on the planet. Having said that, I will also counsel that I have many friends making livings here in their retirements that meet or exceed their burn, meaning they aren't eating into their savings while they live in what they consider to be paradise.

Given the opportunities for creating Web-based businesses, Mexico is a natural for running any sort of Web enterprise. The infrastructure is good, and now with voice-over-IP, any sort of business that can be run over the telephone or the Web can be effectively run from Mexico. That wasn't the case just a few short years ago, but nowadays, the only limitations are your abilities and your imagination. You can have a U.S. number that gets answered in Mexico by you, and nobody will ever be the wiser unless you want to share your secret.

Additionally, any sort of enterprise that leverages an existing skillset you mastered in the U.S. is a fairly good bet. Problem is that if you're going to work in Mexico, you'll need a work visa. Those aren't so easy to get, and I'll cover the ins and outs in a later chapter.

Your best bet is to get a visa that doesn't allow you to take a job in Mexico, and then derive any income from outside the country. Another way of skinning the cat is to have a company here sponsor you as a worker in a field that requires your special expertise. If you're a scofflaw, you could join the ranks of those who are paid entirely in cash and take your chances that you won't get caught; that sounds risky, although reality is that almost nobody ever gets apprehended. Note I'm not condoning that, however. More will follow later in the book, however suffice it to say that where there's a will, there's a way.

The primary orientation of this guide will be to maximize how far your dollar will go, assuming you've already made enough to live on, not that you're going to try to support yourself here. If it's a stretch to find the $1500 to $3000 per month you'll need to live well, this guide won't be of much help, nor will any other guides I've seen, as that's a king's ransom for most Mexicans and it's close to impossible to make that money here. The truth is you are best escaping if your savings can support at least a couple grand a month burn with no serious hit to the principal. If not, you would be best trying to figure out a Web-based or phone-based business to make your money, as the likelihood of it happening in Mexico is slim.

Retiree Living

Retiring in Mexico can be one of the most pleasant and rewarding endeavors of your life. Once you acclimate to the slower pace and the warmer weather, you'll find there are a plethora of activities with which you can pass your time, whether your interests run to fishing, or boating, or off-roading, or painting, socializing, or doing not much of anything at all.

Many retirees start small businesses to keep busy and earn a little extra income. This can run from creating a consulting service based upon your area of expertise, to starting an online business or website. As described earlier, there are many possibilities, and if activity is what interests you, you'll find an endless series of opportunities present themselves as business possibilities. I started a custom home design and construction business in Cabo, and have done quite well. I also started a publishing company to handle my novel writing. I have ownership interest in a restaurant chain that's soon to be a franchise in Mexico. I'm forming an Argentine gelato franchise in Guadalajara that will expand nationally over the next few years.

I retired to Baja to spend time on the beach and on the water, but after four or so months of doing essentially nothing, got bored and decided to start a business to keep busy. That turned into a real company, with dozens of projects now constructed and more in the pipeline. From there I saw opportunities to do something better, or fill a need that wasn't being satisfied, and started businesses to do so, all of which have done well.

Which is to say that if you want to, you can just hang out in a hammock all day, soak up the rays, and watch the world go by. Alternatively, you can keep busy, doing pretty much whatever you can think of. One of my friends volunteers at a local charity to teach English to young Mexicans interested in improving their language skills. Another spends time walking dogs for the local humane society shelter. Still another invests time at a charity book store. Another is taking a "Speak Spanish like a native" course. Another is learning how to make pottery.

Some of my acquaintances who are more vocationally-minded have developed everything from charter operations, to metal fabrication shops, to bars and restaurants. One is exploring getting into the tequila business. Another does interior design, and travels to Guadalajara to pick interesting furniture on a regular basis. I've got friends in the wine business, physicians who donate time to the needy; you name it, Mexico's got it.

There's no shortage of ways to stay occupied.

Many retirees spend a fair amount of time exercising, which is easy to do. Hiking, bicycling, kayaking, swimming, golf, tennis, surfing all are readily available and avidly pursued by the expats here. The biggest danger is always the sun, so sunscreen and hydration are critical.

Of course, many retirees also spend a fair amount of time hanging around the local watering holes, sipping margaritas or *cerveza,* shooting the breeze with each other. Animated discussions on global affairs, the local or U.S. economy, politics, etc. can be heard in many cantinas, as older expatriates spend their time contemplating how the world is going to hell in a hand basket. I have several buddies who do nothing more strenuous than walk their dog to the beach for lunch and cold beer. There's no imperative to actually do anything other than exist, so activity is an option, as opposed to a requisite. The point is that whatever your lifestyle, you can pursue your ambitions or lack of them, left in peace to do as you like.

Exploring Mexico is an enjoyable pastime for many retired folks. Areas like the Tequila region of Jalisco, Guadalajara and its surroundings, Puebla for gourmet Mexican food, San Luis Potosi and Oaxaca for cuisine and ecotourism, Mazatlan for seafood and Pacific Riviera ambiance, Puerto Vallarta and Nuevo Vallarta for fun, and on down the Pacific Riviera all the way to Huatulco. For the inclined there's the entire Mayan Riviera that spans from Chetumal to Tulum to Cancun, which offers an entirely different sort of beach and jungle experience.

Retiring in Mexico can be whatever you want it to be, and you're largely only limited by your desires and imagination, and of course, your pocketbook.

Preparing to Pull the Rip Cord

Now that you have a decent overview of why it's a good idea to consider Mexico as your retirement or escape destination, we'll move on to the nitty gritty in the following chapters. Chapter 2 will go into greater detail on the various destinations and their pros and cons, as well as my recommendations for the choicest spots to live based on a number of factors.

Then we'll go through the info you'll need to know in order to prepare for departure, as well as a fairly thorough review of the topics of interest that will come up once you're here.

As I said earlier, the best place to start is by flying down and spending some time in your target areas, familiarizing yourself with the lay of the land. I would also scour the Internet for any information on areas of interest, remembering that most sites try to make their location sound as good as humanly possible in order to sell you something. That's not my purpose in writing this book. I've spent enough time in hellholes described as "charming" or "quaint" or "rustic" by folks trying to pitch their bed & breakfast or eco-tour outfit or fishing charters to appreciate how disappointing misleading Web descriptions can be, and will do my level best in these pages to avoid coloring any area in an overly positive or misleading way. I have no tour or hotel to sell you, no whale watching boat to rent, no restaurant in Baja to get you to try (although I do have my chicken sandwich places in Guadalajara, which are delicious and affordable, hint hint – fair warning). What you'll get as you go through these pages will be my best take on what living here is like, so you'll be forewarned and forearmed when you decide to take the plunge.

Without further ado, let's get to the nuts and bolts, starting with detailed descriptions of the various areas. These will not be as in-depth as you'll get by spending hours researching a town, so consider them grainy photos of areas designed to give you sufficient overview to decide whether they warrant further exploration. This isn't a travel guide, so I'm not going to devote endless pages to favorite restaurants or things to do while on vacation. Instead, you'll get a few pages giving you the high and low points, the key features and any notable attractions, and my take on what a reasonable budget to live there might be. Larger places will get more coverage, as they'll have more of interest.

Chapter 2

–

Locations

I'm going to highlight eight areas I consider some of the best in Mexico, in terms of safety, affordability, lifestyle, and health care. They are very different from one another. For those seeking a beach resort experience, Cabo San Lucas, San Jose del Cabo fit this bill, although they're at the high end of the price curve for just about everything – because they're hugely popular with celebrities and the well-heeled – so if living on a modest budget is your goal, I'd skip past them and continue to the other destinations. For those looking for a cosmopolitan experience that is European in feel – a cross between Beverly Hills and Florence, say, replete with sidewalk cafes and upscale everything – I highly recommend Zapopan, which is a suburb of Guadalajara. For colonial cities with vibrant cultural heritage, there are Merida, in the Yucatan, and Queretaro, in Queretaro. For greater affordability with all the amenities, there's Colima, which is a couple of hours southwest of Guadalajara (I own property in Cabo San Lucas, Zapopan, and Colima, so I'm clearly biased in their favor). And for those who want an expat lifestyle surrounded by fellow Gringos of a certain age, there's Lake Chapala, about an hour and a half south of Guadalajara, as well as Todos Santos, an hour or so north of Cabo. I'll start with southern Baja, with Todos Santos, and Cabo San Lucas/San Jose del Cabo, and then move to mainland, where the real bargains are to be found, in more ways than one. And instead of publishing countless photos, I will link to Tripadvisor for each area, where thousands of user images can be found to give one a sense of place.

Baja

There are numerous choices in Baja, but I'm going to focus on the ones that are the most accessible and user friendly. I'm omitting La Paz, which is the largest city in Baja California Sur, due to weather (it can get 118 in the summer) and safety (being a larger town, you have more crime, although most of it non-violent) concerns, and Ensenada due to weather (it's blanketed in a marine layer months out of the year in the summer, when everything's sunny in San Diego and Orange County, making it rather gray and dull in my experience) and safety (it's also a larger town, and is too proximate to the border for my liking, which can make it vulnerable to the violence that plagues places like Tijuana). Loreto, which is about a six-hour drive north of Cabo San Lucas, is also not mentioned because I find little to recommend it – there's just not a lot there, and the weather variance is extreme, from near freezing at night in the spring to unbearably hot in summer. That doesn't leave a lot other than the area at the tip of Baja, which includes Todos Santos, Cabo San Lucas, and San Jose del Cabo. Likewise, I'm not going to go into detail on the East Cape area between La Paz and San Jose, because it's pretty barren and desolate, and isn't ideal for anyone but those seeking breathtaking natural beauty without anyone within many miles, including hospitals, or running water, or electricity. So the focus will be the areas that I consider to be habitable, that have access to decent infrastructure and health care, and are safe.

Todos Santos & Pescadero

Todos Santos is a bohemian colonial town built around an oasis of palm trees and fresh water about an hour or so north of Cabo San Lucas. The beaches immediately to the north of the town go for many miles, and the town's borders continue to expand every year.

Todos Santos is a funky place – that's the best descriptor for it. It has some great restaurants, boasts numerous art galleries, and has a number of good hotels, the most prominent being the Hotel California, decked out in rustic mission glory. It's a place with a colonial feel, accentuated by the older mission buildings and the cobblestone streets. While much of Baja is relatively recently built-out, Todos Santos has the gestalt of a town that's been there for centuries. It's home to a thriving and growing artistic group of expats who like the flavor of the area, and its growth shows no signs of slowing any time soon. With a population of six thousand or so, it's an attractive choice for expats seeking an artistic ambiance with good amenities. Because it's an hour drive from either La Paz or Cabo, access to plentiful consumer goods is easy, making it more expat friendly than more isolated areas. Crime is basically unheard of other than petty theft and the occasional opportunistic break-in of an empty home.

Todos Santos hosts art, film and music festivals every year, and regularly gets throngs of tourists looking for something a bit off the beaten path. The community has a small hospital/clinic for basic health care, and also has at least one doctor and dentist in full time residency. Most go to La Paz or Cabo for more critical care, however the locals are fine for mundanities. There are a couple of banks in town, several Pemex stations, and plenty of ATMs and Internet cafes. The main street is lined with cafes and bookstores and little shops, and the town square and church are picturesque and quaint.

Cost to live in Todos Santos is in the couple grand a month range, with more obviously being better. Could you do it on $1500? Probably, but you could also do it on $5K – there are plenty doing it at both ends of the spectrum. One note is that the weather here is markedly cooler than on the Sea of Cortez side, with the population wearing coats and sweaters in the winter, and with summers ten degrees cooler than Cabo or La Paz even in the hottest periods of the summer months. Because of this more dynamic seasonality, many expats prefer the town if they tire of the endless summer characteristics of Cabo, La Paz and the East Cape.

A big downside is there's no hospital, so you have a heart attack or fall down the stairs, you're pretty much screwed. This is a big concern for older folks, so not a matter to treat lightly. The infrastructure is also fairly rustic, which is a polite word for primitive, so if you're not comfortable in that sort of an environment, or you bore easily, you won't like it. Todos Santos is a place for someone looking for serious tranquility, as not much happens. It's a "Pueblo Magico", which is the Mexican equivalent of a cultural heritage site. Whenever I want a weekend getaway with nothing demanding my attention other than staring at my navel, Todos Santos is the ticket.

As you exit the main town and continue down the coast, about ten minutes south of Todos Santos is the smallish agricultural town of Pescadero. Featuring a Pemex station and a handful of small markets and cafes/restaurants, Pescadero has breathtaking beaches with a smattering of homes salted between the large farming tracts. It's an outpost taken straight out of the Sixties, complete with hippie vibe and reggae beat. Laid back is taken to a whole new level, as Todos Santos is the fast-paced neighbor – and it's about a third the speed of La Paz. Type A personalities would be best advised to look elsewhere than Pescadero.

Pescadero has quite a few expats, although I would be surprised to find any rentals. Mostly, it's still affordable land upon which one could build a home. But you never know – you can always check online to see if anyone has anything available.

Costs for Pescadero would be $1200 to $2000, but it would only be suitable for those seeking seclusion. If you think of it as a suburb of Todos Santos, that's probably the most accurate picture. Infrastructure is limited, although most of the area has power, water and phone service with Internet.

About five minutes further south from Pescadero is a condo development on Cerritos beach, featuring a bar and restaurant that has a band every weekend. Some ocean view lots are also being sold, so it's possible that this area will become a viable suburb of Pescadero/Todos Santos in the near future.

- Affordability: 3.8 stars
- Climate: 3.7 stars
- Safety: 4.5 stars
- Healthcare: 3 stars
- Technology accessibility: 3.5 stars
- Accessibility (Time to get to a major U.S. city): San Diego, 1hr drive to La Paz or 1.3 hr drive to San Jose Del Cabo, 2 hrs flight from the airport
- High temperature in Summer: 92 F
- Low temperature in Winter: 54 F at night

Photos of the area: tripadvisor.com/LocationPhotos-g150777-w2-Todos_Santos_Baja_California.html

San Jose del Cabo

At the far southern end of the Baja peninsula lies the town of San Jose del Cabo, and its sister Cabo San Lucas. San Jose del Cabo is one of the original mission towns in Baja, and has grown from a quaint village into a bustling smaller city with a population of around a hundred and twenty-five thousand. Originally settled as a mission in 1730, the city center and surrounding areas have a quaint, colonial feel, more akin to mainland Mexico than Baja. The town is home to the first golf course in southern Baja, although there are now numerous courses from all the top names salted around the area. English is spoken in all of the tourist sections and there is a large and growing expat community of surprisingly diverse composition – everything from retired Canadian and Americans living off social security, to captains of industry living in $30 million beach villas.

San Jose has a thriving dining scene, and has dozens of world class restaurants, from the top of the pricing curve all the way to the affordable-for-the-locals variety. This isn't a cheap town, and prices tend to run thirty percent or so more than in La Paz for food and drink, with property values running in the hundreds of percents higher than anywhere else but Cabo. On the outskirts of town, three communities, Palmilla, Querencia and El Dorado, are flagship big money developments built around world famous golf courses, and homes can be as expensive as the priciest areas of the U.S. More than a handful of internationally famous supermodels, film and music stars have homes in these neighborhoods. Puerto Los Cabos, on the East Cape side of San Jose, is another growing development with stellar prospects – it features a large marina, and its hills are alive with construction of breathtaking villas.

For more reasonable housing, there's everything from row houses in town running from $40K and up (not something I'd recommend), to condos aplenty in virtually every price range, to plots of land in new golf course developments appealing to the more modest budget. Rentals are relatively abundant and a condo in a decent area could run anywhere from $800, to $2500 and up in a marquis community. A reasonable budget for a comfortable lifestyle in San Jose would be in the $2500 to $5000 area for a couple, depending upon your tastes and your housing. You'll want your own vehicle, as the town is pretty spread out, running from the international airport approximately seven miles from the city center to Cerro Colorado, nine miles in the opposite direction from the city center. Bus service is reliable and frequent, however it can get unpleasantly hot in the non-air conditioned buses in the summer, thus isn't practical for most seeking comfort in their everyday existence. The downtown area centers around the church and the main square, and is built about a mile from the nearest beach. In that neighborhood, myriad high-end dining establishments, bars, cafes, art galleries, furniture stores, and clothing shops can be found, although to get to the larger shopping centers dominated by the appropriately named Mega, and Soriana, and Ley's, one needs to venture a mile or two from downtown.

San Jose features some of the nicest beaches in all Baja, and offers good surfing, scuba diving, fishing, and swimming. Of note is that the main beach in the hotel zone isn't safe for swimming, however the Costa Azul beach west of it that stretches for miles is breathtakingly beautiful and has one of the more popular surf breaks outside of the East Cape, which really starts on the northeast side of the Puerto Los Cabos development. The road up the East Cape coast from Puerto Los Cabos leads to a string of unbelievably stunning beaches for many, many miles, starting with the enclave in Zacatecas and continuing north.

Fishing in San Jose is world class, with every variety of marlin mere yards off the coast, as well as swordfish, tuna, dorado, wahoo, rooster fish, shark and rock bass. It's almost impossible not to catch fish in this part of the Sea of Cortez, so if fishing's your hobby, you'll have found heaven. Boats can be chartered out of the small town of La Playita by Puerto Los Cabos, ranging from pangas with outboards to small cabin cruisers.

San Jose is one of those towns that has considerable Gringo influence in terms of creature comforts, with all the usual suspects present in the fast food arena and big box stores, as well as exports like Office Max, Starbucks, etc. etc. etc. There are countless banks, dentists, doctors, beauty salons and massage parlors, and several state-of-the-art hospitals and urgent care clinics. The airport services San Jose and Cabo San Lucas, and is expanding for the third time to accommodate the international and domestic traffic. Two hours from Los Angeles and San Diego, and with direct flights from as far off as New Jersey and Houston, San Jose airport is by far the busiest airport anywhere south of Tijuana in Baja.

San Jose is a little bit of Mexico, a little bit of the States, sort of blended together into an inviting stew. It's quieter than its rowdy sister Cabo San Lucas, and tends to attract an older crowd. Crime is limited to petty theft and the odd burglary, generally in homes that are empty while the owners are in the States, although it suffered a cartel war in 2017 that left a lot of drug dealers dead – which war ended with the new year, and it's been sleepy calm ever since.

All in all, it's hard to beat San Jose for comfort, convenience, amenities, and ambiance. If your budget can support it, it's an absolute must visit for anyone contemplating southern Baja as an expat destination.

- Affordability: 3 stars
- Climate: 4.5 stars
- Safety: 4 stars
- Healthcare: 4 stars
- Technology accessibility: 4.5 stars
- Accessibility (Time to get to a major U.S. city): San Diego, 2 hrs flight
- High temperature in Summer: 100 F
- Low temperature in Winter: 64 F at night

Photos of San Jose del Cabo: tripadvisor.com/LocationPhotos-g152516-San_Jose_del_Cabo_Los_Cabos_Baja_California.html

Cabo San Lucas

Cabo San Lucas, or Cabo to most, is the quintessential cantina town that used to be exclusively the destination of hard-core fisherman, and which has evolved into a world class resort that can hold its own with many of the world's most famous. With a population in the hundred thousand range including the outlying areas, Cabo is vibrant, fun, and unique in all Mexico for its synthesis of the good from the U.S. with the great of Mexico.

The weather is awesome year-round, with the average day in the low eighties and evenings in the high sixties, although it can get humid and hot during hurricane season, which runs from mid-August through end of October. The town is home to the most expensive marina in North America, where a fifty-footer is on the smallish size and where it's not unusual to see dozens of hundred-footers jockeying for spots. It's a place that made its reputation from fishing and partying, and both seminal activities still play a large part in the main tourist area. Cabo is more La Jolla or San Diego than it is Mexico in many ways, and it's one of the places where Spanish is optional rather than a requisite. Gringos abound, and there's a large expat community, again, as with San Jose, ranging from retirees living in small condos on the outskirts, to gazillonaires in twenty-thousand-foot homes on the hill in Pedregal.

Cabo is home to world famous clubs like Cabo Wabo, Squid Roe, Mocambo, and dozens of others. If it's nightlife you're looking for, you found it – every night is Saturday night in Cabo, and it's not unusual to see crowds on the streets at two AM on any given night. The dining is about as good as it gets anywhere, with stunning Italian, Argentine, Sushi, Mexican, Continental, and every other variety of cuisine. Prices are on the higher side, in many places on par with the States, and in some cases, considerably more than anywhere else in Mexico. But that doesn't mean you need to blow a bankroll to live there, it just means you need to be sensible about where you eat and drink. Just as in the U.S., if you live anywhere near a tourist area you probably don't go to the tourist traps. Same applies for Cabo. Some of the best restaurants are two blocks off the main drag – a reliable rule of thumb in most larger towns in Baja.

Cabo has several big box stores – Costco and City Club – and most large chains are represented here, with WalMart, Office Depot, Home Depot, Office Max, McDonalds, Burger King, Domino's, Subway, Starbucks all to be found within a few miles. Gone are the times just a few years back when you only had a few supermarkets to choose from and consumer goods were scarce. Nowadays, you can find anything you could find in the States in Cabo, so from a creature comfort and convenience standpoint it's close to equivalent. There's a massive shopping mall downtown built around the harbor, with names like Tumi and Coach rubbing shoulders with eyeglass stores and cinemas, and more cafes and ice cream parlors and watering holes than imaginable. For wine enthusiasts, there are several competing stores offering hundreds of delectable wines from all over the world, as well as gourmet deli goods and hard to find ethnic specialties. And go up the hill a few miles from the tourist area, and there's another mall that's the equivalent to many you'd find in mid-sized U.S. cities.

Medano beach is a spectacular white sand crescent facing the landmark arch of Land's End. Every variety of watersport is available there, from glass bottom boats to jet skis to parasailing to swimming to banana boat rides. A host of restaurants line the beach offering relatively inexpensive drink specials and passable food, as well as all the bikini watching one could wish for. A Cabo lifestyle is a Hawaiian shirt and flip flop lifestyle, and locals and tourists alike can be found at the beach enjoying the passing scenery.

Cabo is easily the most expensive area of Baja, with a sensible budget in the $2500 to $6000 range, or higher, depending upon what you're looking for. Rentals are plentiful, and you can get anything from a one-bedroom apartment in a local neighborhood for around $400 to $500 per month (I wouldn't do this, but they're available), to two-bedroom condos in guard gated communities in the $1200 to $1700 range, to stand-alone homes from $1800 to $10,000 per month and up. There is a multiple listing service for real estate for sale, however for rentals, you're best advised to ask about realtors who handle rentals, as most don't.

When looking at other costs, some services, like a maid, are reasonable compared to the States, with a full-time person running $500 or less, a part-time person in the $5-$6 per hour range, and a gardener running in the neighborhood of $100 per month or so, depending upon the area to be maintained. A beer on the marina or beach will run $3 or more depending on the place, with it dropping to maybe $2 during happy hour. The same beer in a convenience store would be less than a dollar, and often more like seventy-five cents. A burger on the water could run $10 with an ocean view, and considerably less off the water – but come on, you're at the beach, so pony up for the scenery!

Doctors are also reasonable, with a visit generally costing $30 to $50, depending upon the specialist. For quick fixes and colds, there are some doctors charging $5 or $10 as you move into the locals neighborhoods. Dentists will run around $50 for most procedures, which is expensive by Mexican standards but cheap by Gringo pricing. There are a half dozen hospitals in the area, including a large social security facility, and U.S. prescription medicines are generally available without a prescription in Mexico, at fifty percent or less than U.S. pricing. An important caveat is that brand new medicines, as in on or two years on the market, can be very hard to find and as pricey as in the U.S., reason being that the manufacturers are still making top dollar worldwide on the new meds to recoup their R&D investment.

You don't need a car in Cabo but you'll probably want one, as even though the bus system is incredibly robust and inexpensive (about forty-five cents as of this writing) many of the areas frequented by Gringos are out of town a bit, on the corridor between San Jose and Cabo. One caution is that oftentimes, drivers after dark and on weekends may have had a few *cervezas* or tequila shots, so it's best to drive defensively at all times. It's not unknown for confused motorists to be going the wrong way down one-way streets, or even the wrong way on major arteries – and not always just drunk locals. Many a tourist has gotten baffled by non-existent signage and turned the wrong way down a one-way street, or tried to make a right turn from the far-left lane, apropos of nothing.

Crime in Cabo, as in all Southern Baja, is largely confined to pick-pocketing or burglary or car break-ins. The few murders are almost always drug-related. The town is generally safer than any of the numerous American cities I've spent time in. Having said that, don't go into the barrio waving a wad of hundreds while wearing a Rolex or you'll discover that preying on fools is universal.

Both San Jose and Cabo, and to a lesser degree Todos Santos, are in a hurricane zone, and get slammed with some regularity. Most of the time they are Cat 1 or 2, which don't do much damage other than flooding, but occasionally a really big one hits, like Odile in 2014, which I lived through and knocked out all power and water for weeks. For that reason I recommend hurricane protection, backup generators, and a serious plan B if you're planning to stay to ride one out. Trust me, day 7 without power or water is no picnic, although it's a trip to Club Med compared to day 14 without it. You should also pay close attention to anything you buy or build, because some places get destroyed, whereas others weather the storm well. My home lost roof tile and some paint that looked like it had been sandblasted by the 175 MPH sustained winds, but others in my hood lost garage doors, all their doors and windows, and were gutted as those winds blew through the houses for three or four hours. Trust me you don't want that, especially with the accompanying water damage. An ounce of prevention is worth a fortune in that case.

A question that always arises is "can you drink the water?" In Baja, the answer is yes, as it's all well water, and tests clean. Do I? I don't mind brushing my teeth with it, but I still drink bottled, as I have no idea what is going on with the pipes that bring it to my house, and I don't like rolling the dice to save a few bucks a month.

When everything is taken into account and you've weighed the positives and negatives, if you can afford the place, Cabo is the ideal locale for a premium Baja experience with a healthy dose of fine dining, nightlife, and every imaginable comfort and service. It's highly recommended for a premium beachside existence, and is worth serious consideration if you've squirreled away sufficient nuts to be able to pay the freight on an ongoing basis. That said, if you're careful about your expenditures you can live relatively frugally, but as with everything, if money is an issue I'd advise you to look to mainland, where costs are going to be 30-40% lower, on average, depending on the locale.

- Affordability: 2 stars
- Climate: 4.5 stars
- Safety: 4 stars
- Healthcare: 4 stars
- Technology accessibility: 5 stars
- Accessibility (Time to get to a major U.S. city): San Diego, 2 hrs flight
- High temperature in Summer: 98 F
- Low temperature in Winter: 65 F at night

Photos of Cabo San Lucas:
tripadvisor.com/LocationPhotos-g152515-Cabo_San_Lucas_Los_Cabos_Baja_California.html

Baja Summary

Baja affords the adventurous gringo a plethora of possible settling spots, from quaint and picturesque villages to well-developed cities. Crime is low, the weather is generally good, the areas vary from dirt cheap to moderately expensive, and the entire region is seeing massive investments in infrastructure and consumer goods distribution. Most desirable areas already have significant expat populations, and the locals are easy-going and appreciative of the influx of prosperity Gringos bring to the table. Anyone considering a life outside the U.S. or Canada would do well to explore the regions that sound the most appealing, as well as chatting with expats who've already made the move.

I'm biased, as I've been living in Baja off and on for sixteen years, with more of my time lately spent in Zapopan and Colima. That's not to say Baja's perfect for everyone, but I'd argue forcefully that anyone looking for a relaxed beach lifestyle in an area with good climate and amenable culture would be hard pressed to find anywhere better.

Mainland Mexico

I've traveled all over mainland, and my favorite spots are, without question, Zapopan, which is a northern suburb of Guadalajara (located a five hour drive to Puerto Vallarta in the mountains), and Colima, which is about a hundred miles southwest of Guadalajara, also in the lower reaches of the mountains, and a forty-five-minute drive to the beach. I also like Lake Chapala, although not as much as Colima and Zapopan, and Merida, in the Yucatan, which offers good value but can get seriously hot and humid most months. And I'm also a fan of Queretaro City, about two and a half hours north of Mexico City, which is a nice colonial city that's safe and welcoming. I'll start with Zapopan, and then move to Lake Chapala, and then to Queretaro and Merida, before I finish with what I consider to be the best overall spot in Mexico for my tastes – Colima.

Zapopan, Jalisco

Situated at 5500 feet of elevation, on the northern side of Guadalajara (Mexico's second largest city) lies Zapopan, a 100 square mile suburb that contains some of the most rarefied enclaves in Mexico. If fine dining and luxury lifestyle is your thing, the Andares section of Zapopan is world class and reminds me very much of Beverly Hills. A few blocks from my house there are Ferrari, Mercedes, BMW, Porsche dealers, and thirty or so of the best restaurants in Mexico, as well as one of the nicest malls, which features brands like Hugo Boss, Vuitton, Rolex, Cartier, Tiffany's, and every other top name you can imagine.

The area is home to some of the wealthiest folks in the country, including politicians, business moguls, and the families of those who earned their money in less savory manners. It isn't unusual to see G-Wagons, McLarens, Lambos, and Teslas parked side by side, while a veritable fashion show of the privileged dines at indoor/outdoor restaurants.

For an idea of the gestalt of the place, you can find vids on Youtube that feature The Landmark Guadalajara or Puerta de Hierro, with some of the most expensive real estate outside of Mexico City. These are the wealthy enclaves, but even so the prices are a quarter of what similar areas of the U.S. would cost, and so represent a bargain for the level of lifestyle. Here are a few that will give you a sense of the area:

youtube.com/watch?v=3DaIJNkOmp0&t=50s
youtube.com/watch?v=NMdH1mezB_o
youtube.com/watch?v=ozMlaoPIbhI
youtube.com/watch?v=yntBW2L_vTM

Some of the top hospitals in Latin America are a stone's throw away, with doctors trained at U.S. and European hospitals. Zapopan also has the honor of being the plastic surgery capital of Mexico, which is evident by the folks strolling by with perfectly sculpted features and physiques to die for.

If you're getting the sense that the Andares area is Malibu crossed with Bel Air and Beverly Hills, you aren't too far off. Even from the air it's distinctive, with the fifty story Hyatt Regency at the end of a large cluster of luxury high rises that have more in common with Singapore or Hong Kong than Mexico.

Real Estate is on the pricey side for mainland, with a two-bedroom condo in a high-end building running $300-$500K, and larger units clocking in at a million or more. Single family homes in guard-gated communities will start at $400K for a 25-year-old modest 3 bedroom to well into the millions for mansions in Puerta de Hierro and Zotogrande. That said, homes five to ten minutes away drop to more like $250-$350K, although there are many communities that are now pricing in the $1 million and up range. I use Inmuebles24.com to look at real estate online, and found the lot I built on there, however there are other online services I'd recommend asking around about. Trovit.com.mx is another popular one, but there are more popping up all the time.

Oddly, the rental market is inefficient, and a nice two-bedroom condo can be had for a grand or so a month, with a three-bedroom older home for maybe $1500. I think the reason is that the rents are high for working Mexicans, and if you're wealthy enough to live there, you probably bought a home rather than renting. So there's a disconnect that can be exploited in terms of depressed rental prices in luxury areas, and I have many friends in the area who have been renting for years because the cost works out to be far less than owning, but with all the same amenities. You are advised to find a broker who handles rentals, although because it's a larger city, the online sites will feature many of the available rentals.

Jalisco is a seismic area, so you can expect periodic earthquakes, although not the huge devastating ones that hit Mexico City. I've been through several, that were in the 4 to mid-5 scale, and while things shook, there was no damage. It's more of an uncomfortable nuisance than an existential threat, although one you need to be aware of if you build or buy, or are thinking that 33rd floor penthouse's amazing view is worth the swaying when one hits. Because it's inland and in the mountains you don't have to worry about hurricanes, although hail storms in the summer months are a thing, and can ding up a car left outside pretty well – so covered parking is a must.

Food and drink are laughably inexpensive – typically 25% or so less than Cabo, which is maybe 40% less than the US. A nice lunch at a top restaurant might cost $5-$7, and dinner in the millionaire's row spots could be $10-$20 for dinner, depending on how you order. But that would be white tablecloths and suited wait staff in the most popular places. If you venture a few minutes away prices will drop by another 20%. By Mexican standards that's expensive, but a friend of mine who comes and visits periodically is always amazed when four of us go to the best steak place in the zone, drink a few bottles of wine, and walk out of the place for $120, tops. He's fond of telling me an equivalent dinner in San Diego, where he lives, would be $500, easy (and his condo costs $7500 a month downtown, versus a similar place in Zapopan being more like $1500 a stone's throw from the restaurant and mall strip). In short, the Andares area is top shelf all the way, and can successfully compare to the

Fashion Island or South Coast Plaza areas of Orange County, Westwood or Beverly Hills in Los Angeles, or similar U.S. platinum level districts, and a fraction of the price.

I have a friend who rents a home in Puerta de Hierro, which is one of the premier guard-gated and patrolled communities in Andares, and he pays $1400 a month for his three-bedroom home, which would sell for $400-$500K. His cost of living for his girlfriend, kid, and himself, comes to around $50K a year, including a private school, maid, and plentiful top shelf tequila. For the ambience and amenities, that's a bargain, as the same lifestyle in Orange County, where he's from, would be more like $180K and up, post-tax. Ubers cost $1.50-$4 pretty much anywhere in the city, to put transportation into context, although traffic is generally horrible in Guadalajara, especially around rush hour, when it might be faster to walk two miles than drive it. While you don't need a car, you'll probably want one, although most who live in the area walk everywhere, which is part of the draw as well as the premium price.

A nearby party zone is Chapultepec in Guadalajara, where the younger university crowd carouses, and if that's your thing you'll find plentiful $1 beer and $2 shots, catering to the youth clientele. To put things in perspective that same beer in the Andares zone would be more like $2-$2.50, which is still dirt cheap.

Crime in the Andares zone is virtually unheard of. There are four police forces, including a private mall force that carries Uzis. The message to miscreants is not to come to Andares to misbehave, because the guns are loaded and pointed at them, to protect the wealthy residents. I've walked home at three in the morning after a night of celebration and never had any issues, and the zone is famous for being the safest in Mexico, for good reason. Senators, judges, business magnates, and their offspring demand and receive the best of all things, including security, and the entire area has a cultured, safe feel to its manicured grounds.

This is not the Mexico you see in movies, nor is it most Gringos' expectations of Mexico. The vast majority of Mexicans have never heard of it, and even fewer Americans or Canadians have. I only learned of it when I was buying a luxury vehicle there. I flew into Guadalajara airport, which is one of the largest international airports in Mexico, and was blown away by what I saw when I arrived in Zapopan to check out the vehicle. It was like I'd been transported to a different country, one that was totally first world in every respect. I decided to spend serious time there, and after a year of multi-week trips, I bought a lot in one of the communities and built a home – so to say I was impressed was an understatement.

The weather in Guadalajara is mild year-round due to the altitude, with AC only required maybe one month a year (May, the hottest month) – it's in the mountains, so crisp evenings and warm days (75-85 F), with seasonal rains from June through October at night for a few hours. Zapopan is dressier than Baja, as one might imagine, so the flip-flops and Hawaiian shirts that would cut it in Cabo are not going to fly there – jeans, a polo shirt, and at night a jacket would be appropriate for a male, and the equivalent for females.

Private schools are on par with the best in the world, with costs ranging from $350-$800 a month, depending on the school and the grade. Almost all are bilingual, and some are tri-lingual, with the German School having the best academic reputation in the area.

Many speak English in Zapopan due to the education system, so language is rarely an issue. But if it's the company of plentiful Gringos you crave, you won't find many, as most have no idea it exists. Better to go south to Lake Chapala, where expats have been relocating for decades.

The Andares and surrounding area in Zapopan is for those who want to immerse themselves in the best of the best. A reasonable budget for a couple with their own home might be $40K a year ($50-$60K if renting), although you could certainly spend much more, or squeak by on $38-$40K, depending on how often you ate out. It's an area where you wouldn't feel out of place in a Mercedes or wearing a nice watch, although as in any large metro area I wouldn't make a habit of being flashy. That said, the concentration of wealth is conspicuous, and with that comes the security you would expect, so while it's pricier, you're unlikely to find a safer place anywhere on the planet.

As to food and water integrity, I would put the restaurants at US standards of food handling. I'm an owner of a chain of chicken sandwich restaurants in Guadalajara (named Peku, after the sound a Mexican chicken makes in Spanish), one of which is in the Andares area, and we have protocols that are exactly the same as any in the U.S., with employees wearing gloves, masks, washing their hands whenever entering the kitchen, refrigeration and cooking rules stringently adhered to, etc. I've been eating at restaurants in the area for years, and have never once been poisoned, except at, ironically, an

American chain (cough cough Outback cough), where my undercooked burger carried a high price tag (nine hours in the ER came to $400). But that's one experience out of many hundreds (I eat out just about every meal), and I sort of knew better when I saw the burger – but I was starving. As to water, if you have a home filtration system with UV sanitation, you would be fine, but I still order five gallon jugs of water for drinking (I brush my teeth from the tap, and haven't suffered any ill effects, if you don't count the bleeding Elvis-shaped mole growing on my neck), as does everyone I know. At $1.75 per bottle I figure it's the best insurance I can buy, and I'm more than willing to spring for a couple bottles a week – most budgets can handle that. The issue is the same as in over 3000 metro areas in the US: with pipes that could well be over 100 years old, you have no idea what sort of contamination could be leaking into the water system, so best to assume the worst. This goes for all Mexico, except for Cabo, where the water is from wells and routinely tests purer than tap water in the U.S. in the areas where you can actually drink it.

An important caveat is that I never eat off the street. There are myriad carts and street restaurants set up all over every Mexican town, but there isn't a lot of hand washing going on that I can see, and no barrier to dust being blown up by passing cars and settling on the food. I have friends who dine on street food all the time and swear by it, but I also have a friend whose buddy died from parasites picked up from street food in Mexico City, so I prefer to play it safe and give it a miss. For Gringos I would advise to pass on the tacos and whatnot being offered in open air on the street. It's just a bad idea, even if you see crowds around the vendor.

For the record, there are zero street vendors in the Andares area of Zapopan. So this is mainly a cautionary tale for other areas.

If you're big on the idea of expat groups, there are plentiful opportunities to meet other Gringos in Guadalajara. The Chapultepec neighborhood is multicultural and has plentiful exchange students from all over the world attending Guadalajara's world class universities, and there are lots of expat forums online where you can find groups in your area. But if you decide to live near Andares, or in the Providencia district adjacent to it (also nice, but not walking distance from the action), you won't encounter many Gringos or hear much English. It's a genuine secret, even to the vast majority of Mexicans.

No discussion of Zapopan would be complete if the vibrant culture of Guadalajara wasn't mentioned, with theater, ballet, concerts a regular occurrence, and a thriving arts scene. As mentioned earlier, Guadalajara is a university town, so it has the energy of a melting pot of youthful exuberance, with something for every taste, be it civilized evenings of tequila or fine wine tasting, or clubbing till five a.m., or rock concerts in the park, or street markets that feature nightly salsa or swing classes that are well attended by the locals and visitors alike.

For me, Guadalajara has much of the attraction that some of my other favorite cities have – Buenos Aires, Mendoza, Paris, Florence, Lisbon – and you might well believe you were in any one of them were it not for everyone speaking Mexican Spanish. The city has gorgeous architecture and a definite presence that's unlike any other in Mexico, and is considered the most cosmopolitan and cultured in the country – for good reason. In Zapopan, you're twenty or so minutes away from most of Guadalajara's attractions, but distant enough so you don't have to deal with unpleasant urban issues like the homeless, or graffiti, or higher crime.

- Affordability: 2.8 stars
- Climate: 4.5 stars
- Safety: 5 stars
- Healthcare: 5 stars
- Technology accessibility: 5 stars
- Accessibility (Time to get to a major U.S. city): San Diego, 3 hr flight, Dallas and Arizona, 2 hours and change
- High temperature in Summer: 88 F
- Low temperature in Winter: 62 F at night
- Average daily temp 75F year-round. May is the hottest month with days in the low 90's, but cooling off in the evenings. AC only necessary 45 days a year, if that.

Photos of the Andares area of Zapopan:
tripadvisor.com/Attraction_Review-g1006488-d3507776-Reviews-Andares-Zapopan_Guadalajara_Metropolitan_Area.html

Lake Chapala, Jalisco

The expat neighborhoods of Lake Chapala are mainly concentrated in the towns of Ajijic and Chapala, and in the hills of San Juan Cosala, all located on the shores of a 45-mile-wide lake that's about an hour and a half drive from

Guadalajara. The temperature is a bit cooler than Guadalajara during the day, and about the same at night, which is to say pleasant year round due to the elevation and latitude – both Guadalajara and Chapala are roughly the same latitude as Puerto Vallarta, which is tropical, but because of the altitude they're far less humid and hot during the summer.

Ajijic is a quaint, rustic town with cobblestone streets (actually lava rock, but close enough) that meander down to the lakeshore, lined with funky restaurants and art galleries, with a bohemian charm that for many typifies a kind of stereotypical colonial Mexican village. On weekends it's crowded with cars from Guadalajara, but during the week it thins out, and is mostly locals and expats going about their business. With a population of about eleven thousand, Ajijic is the primary expat community of "Lakeside," and just about everyone you'll encounter speaks English, or can snag someone who does. Restaurants that suit virtually any palate or budget abound, and there is truly something for everyone within a stone's throw of the lake.

Housing in Ajijic, which is more desirable than Chapala, runs the gamut from modest to multi-million-dollar homes, with prices increasing the better the view. There are many expats who've built retirement places along the water or in the hills, and any number of developers who've catered to the demand. The majority seem to fall in the $500K and up range, but bargains can still be had if you spend sufficient time on the ground and are willing to consider less popular locations. Prices in Chapala are under half the cost of Ajijic, but for good reason, as expats are rarely interested in living there vs. Ajijic, so the costs are more accessible for locals. The problem being that the build quality and the neighborhoods in Chapala aren't nearly the same, and the bars on the windows of the homes are necessary, not decorative.

Rentals are tight due to the number of expats vying for the same slots, and it's difficult to find anything decent for under $800-$1000 a month. It's a shame, because years ago you could rent the same place for more like $400-$500, but time moves on, and as word has spread about the area's charms, supply and demand have seen rents climbing steadily. Still, by U.S. standards it's a bargain, but it is one of the factors that I've been watching with some disappointment. Is it still a retirement secret, then? Sure. A few thousand expats doesn't mean the cat's out of the bag, but it does mean that if there are only a few hundred apartments that aren't seedy, you're going to pay more for them.

There are a number of private schools in the area, and tuition can range from $100-$350 a month. All that I know of require uniforms, and you'll also be frontloading the costs for books, registration fees, etc. so will take a hit on the cost of admission. After that, it's reasonable for what you get, with many bilingual, and a good academic track record. Do your homework and ask around, and the same names will keep coming up over and over, which is a good indicator for where you'll want to enroll any little ones.

Costs are a bit less than the Andares area, but still higher than places like Merida or Colima. That said, a bottle of scotch is about a quarter the price in Canada and half as much as the U.S., and a pack of cigarettes is a couple of dollars. A bottle of beer in a bar might run $2 or so, and a lunch at a reasonable place could be in the $4-$6 range. Maids are more expensive than other areas of mainland due to the number of expats willing to pay more, but hardly excessive at $400 or so for full time and $5 or so per hour for part-time. I've had nice dinners for $15 per person including a beer at a number of places without too much difficulty in finding prices like that, and if I'm willing to go simpler on ambience and décor, $10. By Mexican standards that is expensive, so more special occasion than anything, but again, we're talking a spot that is used by locals from Guadalajara as a weekend vacation area, so prices will naturally reflect the increased demand. Internet might run 800 pesos a month, or about $35 USD. Cell plans from $5 a month.

A couple could live sparingly on $2000 a month, depending upon rent. $2500 would be a better lifestyle, and $3000 would be ample. If one owned one's own home, $1800-$2000 a month would be ample. Here is a good site with spreadsheets and a breakdown of some typical costs: https://www.accesslakechapala.com/guide/living-costs/

Crime is mainly burglaries, car break-ins, and petty theft, although occasionally there have been bouts of car-jacking and muggings, usually by predators who came over the hill from Guadalajara's seedier areas to prey on the elderly expats. That said, it is best to keep one's wits about you when out, as there are youths who might see a purse as an opportunity, or an open vehicle as an invitation.

The lake itself is a work in progress, and unfortunately suffers from contamination by pesticides to a degree that has rendered it toxic to those who use it to drink from and bathe in. That isn't the expats, but the impoverished locals that live along its shores and use the water for drinking and washing have the highest incidence of renal disease in the world. So while it's nice to look at, I wouldn't advise anyone to go for a swim in the water, and for God's sake don't drink it. That said, there is a major cleanup effort underway, but unfortunately the river that feeds the lake is one of the most polluted in Mexico, and several large outfits along the shore use toxic pesticides that flow to the water when it rains, so if purity of the lake is an issue for you, best to skip it and consider somewhere else.

Ajijic definitely has a kind of village charm as opposed to neighboring Chapala, and is a popular attraction for knowledgeable expats, for a reason. I include it in my book because many love the area and swear by it, and because probably less than 1% of Gringos have actually been there, even if they're exploring places to live on mainland Mexico. More often they'll move somewhere they've vacationed, like PV or Cancun, where they will pay a substantial premium to live in a tourist locale. While pricier than many other mainland destinations, Lake Chapala is still a steal by U.S. and Canadian standards, and because so few have visited it, deserves at least a mention on any list.

Anyone living "Lakeside" will want a car, due to the distances involved in getting anywhere. While taxis are available, I haven't met many who didn't own a vehicle, and I can't see a lifestyle where I didn't have one given the rural nature of the location and Guadalajara only an hour and a half away.

I looked at buying there when I was offered a fire sale a few years back, but passed, because I actually prefer locales where every other person you run into isn't from the old country; and the Lake Chapala area is one where many you encounter are other expats. If that's your thing, it may be right for you. Is it a retirement secret? Like Cabo, it may not be for everyone, but it's unknown enough with the vast majority as a retirement or expatriation destination to qualify as a good choice. Are there other, better secrets out there? A few, which I'll mention shortly (Zapopan is far nicer, IMO, as is Cabo, as you can actually get into the water, even if it's pricier), and still more I won't because I haven't spent enough time in them to recommend them. That's one of the issues with researching online versus actually living in a place for some time – the internet can give one an unbalanced view.

While we're on the topic of close but no cigar, honorable mentions could easily go to Ensenada, which has a fair number of expats but which I've disqualified for weather and safety reasons due to proximity to the border, and La Paz, which I've also chosen not to highlight for weather and general aesthetics, as well as worsening crime over the last few years. On mainland, there are enclaves in Puerto/Nuevo Vallarta, and Mazatlan, as well as up the Pacific coast, but they're pricey for what you get, and also have security concerns, especially Mazatlan, which is in Sinaloa, where the Sinaloa Cartel operates with impunity. I've also spent time in Oaxaca, which is quite colonial and charming but is plagued by large earthquakes, crime, and spotty infrastructure (although it is improving), but can't recommend it as of this writing due to all three concerns, and in San Luis Potosi and Leon and Queretaro, which are also lovely but have legitimate security concerns, even in the better neighborhoods. Tulum and Playa del Carmen have weather issues (hotter than hell much of the year and seriously humid) and security issues due to cartels operating in the area and battling one another for turf. San Miguel de Allende has a large expat population, but has also experienced rising crime from cartels, so I'm giving it a miss until/if that situation improves. Are these areas actively dangerous? For the most part, no (except for Playa del Carmen), but the point is there's more risk, and part of what I'm trying to do is to minimize your risk in moving to Mexico, not put you into a dangerous situation. Should you go check those areas out, if so inclined? Sure, but be aware of the issues I've raised, and don't look at any place through rose colored glasses. Talk to locals who have nothing to sell, and ask plenty of questions.

- Affordability: 3.8 stars
- Climate: 4.5 stars
- Safety: 4.5 stars
- Healthcare: 4 stars (Guadalajara an hour and a half away)
- Technology accessibility: 5 stars
- Accessibility (Time to get to a major U.S. city): San Diego, 3 hr flight, Dallas and Arizona, 2 hours and change
- High temperature in Summer: 84 F
- Low temperature in Winter: 64 F at night
- Average daily temp 75F year-round. Weather is famous for being "eternal Spring."

Photos of Lake Chapala:
tripadvisor.com/Attraction_Review-g1575477-d153217-Reviews-Lake_Chapala-Jalisco.html

Queretaro City, Queretaro

Queretaro City is the fifth fastest growing city in Mexico, with a population of about 750,000 in the metro area. It's a colonial town, with a famous aqueduct running through the middle of it, and a charming downtown area that I find typical of what I think of old-world Mexico. I've spent many a day wandering its streets, sampling its restaurants and shops, and have always felt comfortable and safe there. It is about a two and a half hour drive from Mexico City, and is 40 miles from San Miguel de Allende, which has a large and vocal expat community (although the area has seen its crime and costs spike in the last few years, which is one of the reasons it doesn't make it into this book other than as a mention – that, and it's hardly a secret since it is the topic of numerous books, specials, and videos as an expat haven).

For me, Queretaro has everything one might want for a smallish city (anything less than a million I consider a smallish city), including a rich cultural legacy as one of the primary cradles of Mexican independence. Its downtown area boasts countless colonial buildings and churches, and seems steeped in history, with the ghosts of the past still walking the cobblestone streets, and every other edifice seeming to claim an important role in the independence movement. It has served as the capital of Mexico several times, and is still an important metropolis, with a burgeoning industrial base.

The weather is generally warm and mild year round, with a rainy season from June to October that drops an average of 20 inches per year, and it can get hot in the summer months, as in well over 90 degrees, and can drop into the forties at night in winter due to its altitude, which is over six thousand feet above sea level. For that reason, those with respiratory issues might want to give it a pass, as there's less oxygen at that height, and it can be hard on those with lung problems or O2 deficiency. The historic center of town is a UNESCO World Heritage Site, and its baroque architecture is a popular tourist attraction for Mexicans and foreigners alike.

Housing costs run the gamut from dirt cheap in the less desirable areas, to expensive in the premium communities. Simple apartments can be had for $250 and up (studio) rent in working class communities, but can easily reach the $1000 or more level as you venture into the more desirable districts. Bargains can be had, but they're hard to come by, as housing is at a premium due to the city's rapid growth. To put it into perspective, cost to rent is roughly 10% lower than Zapopan, but 40-60% higher than Colima, and about 30% higher than Merida. A new car will cost between 20-30% more in Queretaro than Colima, and all other costs are roughly in line with those percentages. For that reason, while Queretaro has much to recommend it, I wouldn't put it at the lower end of the cost spectrum, although it does compare favorably to other areas around it, like Mexico City and San Miguel.

Land is at a premium if you're considering buying, and the lot sizes run small, as in a couple thousand square feet, on average. A typical row house in a working class community might start at $100K USD and up, and in a gated community, more like $175K and up, although you're going to be on a postage size lot crammed in with a host of other homes, usually with shared walls, so more glorified townhomes than stand-alone. Places on larger lots in premium locations will start at $400K and easily go to $800K or more pretty quickly, depending on the lot size and the location. So if bargain housing is what you're after, while I love Queretaro for its central location, you'd be better advised to look to Merida or Colima, where your dollar will buy you twice as much.

As to other costs, a meal for two at a mid-level restaurant might run $25-$30 USD (by way of comparison, that might cost more like $15-$17 in Colima or $18-$22 in Merida). Groceries will range anywhere from 15-75% more than Colima or Merida. Power is about 20% more. A beer will be about 15% more. This is all a function of location and demand. As the city grows, salaries are higher than in places with little or no industry like Colima, so everything winds up costing more as the market will bear it. Having said that, it's still inexpensive by U.S. standards, and certainly is less than places like Cabo or PV due to their tourist inflation, so it's not exorbitant, just pricier than the other bargain spots in this book (Merida and Colima being the gold standards for safety and value).

There is an expat community in town, and there are a couple of online groups you can seek out on Facebook by searching Queretaro Expats that are good places to network and get information on local shops, handymen, current events, and so on.

Queretaro is one of the safest cities in Mexico, and crime is typically non-violent property type, so safety isn't an issue if you take reasonable precautions. Recently there has been an uptick in violence due to criminal gangs jockeying for territory, but tourists and expats are left out of their tussles, so at least as of this writing, it is a safe place to live – as safe or safer than most American cities, per numerous web resources.

Good private hospitals abound, and costs are in line with the rest of Mexico, albeit higher than the true bargain spots. And Mexico City is close enough so that if one requires specialized procedures that the local facilities don't inspire confidence in providing, a few hour bus ride or drive and you're in the country's capital of health care.

Like all of Mexico, Queretaro is a seismic area, and earthquakes are not unknown, although the region tends to escape the large, devastating shakes that visit Mexico City periodically. Still, it is an issue to consider when eyeing rentals or considering buying a home, as much of the construction isn't performed with stringent earthquake precautions in mind, and cracking or worse can certainly be an ongoing problem in less expensive or older structures.

The water isn't safe to drink from the tap due to the age of the pipe networks, so plan on drinking bottled water, as is a good idea in all of Mexico other than Baja.

I can't stress enough how charming the historic district is, and how many hours of pleasant days I have spent wandering its streets and sipping coffee at its sidewalk cafes. It is filled with gorgeous churches, museums, cultural heritage sites, plazas, and theaters, and if immersing yourself in colonial splendor is your thing, it's a perfect location. I recommend it over other locales that nearly made this book, like Aguascalientes (which is a nice city, but has no real attractive qualities that make it stand out from a dozen others to my eye), or Oaxaca, due to its cultural attractions and its relatively benign earthquakes (I love Oaxaca, but can't recommend a destination where the city can be shut down for a week due to an earthquake, as has happened recently in Oaxaca, or where it rains a lot – I lived in the SF Bay area, and have had enough of constant rain to last a lifetime. If catastrophic shakers and lots of rain don't trouble you, I would definitely take a look at Oaxaca city as well). Queretaro is definitely a good option if you don't mind paying a premium for it compared to my final pair of recommended cities, as it has many fine qualities, including the second largest wine producing region in Mexico, relatively modern infrastructure (internet, cell, roads), and a plethora of good restaurants (although not the gourmet smorgasbord of places San Miguel de Allende boasts). In other words it is a solid candidate with plenty of charm most Gringos don't know exists, and if you're a couple that can spend $30-$40K a year for a nice lifestyle, it's definitely recommended.

- Affordability: 3.5 stars
- Climate: 4.25 stars
- Safety: 5 stars
- Safety: 5 stars
- Healthcare: 4.5 stars
- Technology accessibility: 5 stars
- Accessibility (Time to get to a major U.S. city): 3 hours on average via Mexico City Airport
- High temperature in Summer: 84 F
- Low temperature in Winter: 40 F at night
- Average daily temp 70-80F year-round.

Photos of Queretaro:
tripadvisor.com/LocationPhotos-g479232-Queretaro_City_Central_Mexico_and_Gulf_Coast.html#36583460

Merida, Yucatan

Most have heard of the Yucatan because of the Mayan ruins of Chichen Itza, or its proximity to Cancun and Cozumel, which are in Quintana Roo. But its state capital, Merida, is a genuine secret like Zapopan or Colima, and is worth a hard look, depending upon taste. It's hot year-round, with average daily highs in the 90-100 Fahrenheit range and nights around 70, so if you don't enjoy humid heat, you can skip it. Ditto for rain, as it receives about 41 inches of rain each year, which contributes to its humidity, although it's seasonal and usually takes place in the evening. But make no mistake, it's the jungle, which means you'll be contending with the usual assortment of critters, including mosquitoes, lizards, spiders, and everything else you'd expect in a tropical clime. And even though it's only about 20 miles from the beach, it doesn't get much of a cooling breeze – think Florida or Houston in the summer, only worse.

That said, the city is vibrant, if seriously laid back, and relaxation and the afternoon siesta are mainstays of the culture. Its colonial city center is picture book typical for the region, with a main square and plentiful churches and formidable government buildings, many of which are painted in vibrant pastels that make for a charming aesthetic. While many expats have gravitated to one of the suburbs that continue to pop up to the north of the city (Las Americas, Carcel, etc.), or one of the golf course communities for guard gated resort living, still others have taken to renovating century-old homes in the downtown area – a prospect that isn't for the faint of heart or those on a limited budget. A good rule of thumb is the further north you go in Merida, the more affluent the area. And anywhere with the word "Monte" in the title is going to be nicer. When expats move to Merida, they will largely choose one of the Montes after looking over their options, at least for rentals. The downside is that you're a decent distance from the city center, so if you're after that vibrant experience, you're going to be paying a lot of ubers, or spending a fair amount of time behind the wheel.

There is a significant presence of wealthy Mexican retirees in Merida, as well as all types of expats, but the majority of the population is of modest means, so there is definitely a palpable class difference in every interaction. Where many areas in Mexico the population is usually polite, in Merida it's not unusual for the more prosperous to look down their noses at the service class, and treat them accordingly. This is different than any of the other places I've recommended, and is somewhat odd, but seems to be a cultural norm, if an unattractive one.

Progreso beach is a 20-mile run north from the city, and there are numerous marinas just west of it in Puerto de Abrigo, if boating is your thing. The beaches can get crowded on weekends, as can the restaurants, when the city empties out in an attempt to get relief from the ever-present heat. But proximity to the Gulf of Mexico means all the fresh seafood you can eat, so if you like fish or shellfish, you're in luck.

Healthcare is widely available at good hospitals, which range from the IMSS public facility, to higher end private hospitals with sparkling interiors and all the latest gear. Acceptance of Gringo health insurance is spotty, at best, so if you're going to relocate, I recommend buying the Mexican variety, as it is inexpensive and worth the peace of mind. Having said that, I don't carry it for myself, because out of pocket costs are so low for anything but a major emergency it's just not a good buy, but don't do as I do, do as I say and sleep well at night, especially if you have any underlying conditions. I'll cover insurance options in a later chapter.

Real Estate is reasonably priced, depending on where you look. If a boxy row house in a newer suburb is acceptable, there are plenty to choose from starting from $100K – but you get what you pay for in terms of construction quality, and it's not unusual for those places to start falling apart once the keys are handed over. In the nicer areas, like the golf course communities, you can easily start at $400K and go up from there, with some larger homes in the $600K-$1 million plus range. As with most things, there are no free lunches, and you'll generally get what you pay for, so I advise to pay serious attention to construction quality as well as the neighborhood, with an eye to what it's likely to wear like over the next decade or two.

One negative, at least for many Gringos, and certainly for resale, is that most Mexican homes are contemporary style and two story, with the living area down, and the bedrooms up. While not a big deal if you're fit and in your thirties or forties, as folks age they generally gravitate to a single level living plan so their knees don't take a battering, they don't risk a slip and fall, and they can easily get to their bedroom without hiking up 20 or more steps multiple times a day. Mexicans don't seem to mind this, but most Gringos I've spoken with prefer no stairs, so keep that in the forefront when evaluating costs – you'll likely only be able to sell your two story box to a Mexican whenever it comes time, which will inevitably impact the resale value as they tend to want bargains when home shopping.

You'll want a broker, or multiple brokers, because there's no MLS, although Inmuebles24.com has plenty of listings. The problem being that the best deals are often not widely advertised because the brokers are reluctant to split commissions with another agent, so it's hit or miss with what they've kept as "pocket listings" for only their clients.

Rentals are plentiful and cheap, with apartments or modest homes starting in the $400 and up range, but again, it depends on what your expectations are. If you want to live around others who can only afford a nominal rent, with all that implies about neighborhoods, noise, quality of life, etc. then you can certainly find cheap options, but I'd advise going upstream on costs and budgeting at least $700-$800 for a rental in a nicer area.

Internet is fast and relatively inexpensive at $30 a month or so. What will eat you alive in Merida is electric, because air conditioning is absolutely mandatory, and you'll burn a ton of electricity cooling your home. CFE, which is the national power company, is subsidized at lower consumption levels, but once you move beyond what you'd use with only a few fans and a refrigerator it will start to get expensive, as in hundreds of dollars a month. This is also a concern in Cabo, where AC is required half the year, but while an expensive proposition there, it's triple that in Merida, where you'll melt without AC running 24/7. I've seen bills of five hundred or more per month for a decent size house, so you should ask to see an electric bill for past renters before signing, as older equipment can cost far more than newer to operate, and you may be signing up to a massive unexpected cost you never saw coming.

If you are going to buy or build, I can't recommend solar highly enough. Most companies can hook up your array so it feeds any excess power generated back to the grid, and it can lower your bills by 80% or more, paying for itself in four years or so, depending on what you use without it.

Merida is in a hurricane zone, so that's a real concern in terms of loss of power, and damage from both high winds, and torrential rain. It gets hit by big ones periodically, so if you decide to live there, during the season it is a natural disaster waiting to happen. The point being that you need to stormproof your house, and be prepared to cook in hundred-degree heat for days without power if a big one decimates the area. I would recommend two weeks' worth of water and food, and a propane backup generator or bulletproof solar, at the minimum.

Food costs are bargain basement, with a good lunch in the $3-$4 range at a variety of quality restaurants, and $7-$12 for a nice dinner in a popular place. Drinks are similarly inexpensive, with beer running a buck or two in a bar or restaurant, and cocktails only a bit more. If you're aspiring to develop a serious alcohol problem, either Merida or Colima are your ticket, because it's hard to spend $10 for a few hours out slamming back cold ones. Likewise, if you eat at home you might spend a few hundred bucks for a couple – however my philosophy is with restaurants so cheap, it almost doesn't make sense to cook yourself unless it's something you really enjoy.

Rideshare services like Uber and Didi are ubiquitous in Merida, however if you live anywhere but the city center, you'll want a car. There are a number of new car dealers in town, as well as plentiful used lots. Gasoline all over Mexico is priced similarly, and is about the same as in the U.S. per gallon.

For bang for the buck, the two hands-down winners in this book are Merida, and Colima. The negative with Merida, as I've alluded to, is the weather, which includes the heat and the hurricanes. If those don't faze you, then it's worth giving it a serious look, because for value it's hard to beat, although of the pair I prefer Colima for the weather and the lack of large storm danger. In Merida, a couple of grand a month for a couple would be adequate to enjoy a nice lifestyle, assuming a modest rent and not a ton of AC use. If you own a home, that couple of grand would be more than adequate, although just a bit more would have you living like a high roller.

Crime is virtually unheard of in Merida, which is billed as the safest city in Mexico. This is especially true if you live in one of the gated communities, which add a further level of insulation from opportunistic crime. Most of what I've heard about are burglaries on empty homes, and petty theft, which you'll find anywhere in the world. I've never felt endangered there, which is another reason it makes my list – at a certain age, I don't need drama, and I certainly don't need to be worried about my possessions or my safety. Merida ticks the security box in a big way.

Private schools are on par with the rest of the locales I've features, with costs ranging from $100-$300 a month, depending on the school and the grade. Many are bilingual, and everyone I've talked to who has their kids in a private school has had nothing but good things to say about the experience.

English is widely spoken in the more cosmopolitan areas, however you would do well to learn at least some of the language so you can interact seamlessly on basic discussions like getting gas, ordering in a restaurant, instructing a handyman, talking to a maid, getting a haircut, and so on. You could get by with no Spanish, but it isn't advised, and it's worth at least trying, in my experience.

There are plenty of smaller shops that will provide for virtually any need, as well as big box stores and large malls, so creature comforts and consumer goods are widely available and reasonably priced. There are also niceties like premium movie theaters (with full bars and food service from a menu), and a seemingly never-ending procession of fiestas to keep you busy. However relaxation is a big draw for the area, and swinging in a hammock is considered as valid a use of one's time as typing out a new novel. No comment on how I'd know that.

The tap water is safe to drink, however with a major caveat, which is that testing occurs at the treatment level, before it flows through the pipes to wherever you are. There's no telling what bacteria can enter those pipes on the run to your place, so as with all areas of Mexico, I tend to err on the side of caution and recommend 5 gallon bottles of water for drinking, as mentioned in other sections. The tap water is also relatively mineral heavy, so could cause problems with your kidneys if you drank it long term, so I wouldn't – just spring the couple bucks a week and get the big bottles.

There's no street food in Merida, other than something called a marquesita, which is like a crepe, only crunchier, with melted cheese or Nutella, but even those require permits and sanitation check-ups.

Merida has a number of museums and cultural activities, including a symphony orchestra.

There are many expat internet groups and plentiful videos on YouTube about life in Merida. Anyone seriously considering it as a relocation option should spend some time researching before hopping on a plane. It has much to recommend it, with the only major drawback for me being the weather, as well as the distance from major metro areas like Guadalajara and Mexico City. It does have an international airport with good flight availability to the rest of Mexico as well as the U.S., so travel to and from is painless and easy, if not cheap. It's worth a serious look if you're on a budget, want to maximize your lifestyle, and can handle the heat and humidity.

- Affordability: 4.8 stars
- Climate: 2.3 stars
- Safety: 5 stars
- Healthcare: 4.5 stars
- Technology accessibility: 5 stars
- Accessibility (Time to get to a major U.S. city): 1.5-2 hours to Florida, Texas, Deep South
- High temperature in Summer: 100+ F
- Low temperature in Winter: 75 F at night
- Average daily temp 95F year-round. AC is a must year-round.

Photos of Merida:
tripadvisor.com/LocationPhotos-g150811-Merida_Yucatan_Peninsula.html

Colima, Colima

Nestled between Lake Chapala and the Pacific coast is a hidden gem most Mexicans are unaware exists, and most Gringos have never heard of: Colima, the capital city of Colima state. With a population of about 200K it has a small-town feel, with none of the traffic or pollution of a larger metropolis but all the amenities thanks to it being the capital. Situated at an elevation of approximately 1500 feet, it enjoys year-round weather of 75-80 during the day and 60-70 at night, with rain many early evenings that cool things off (think Hawaii, but less humid). It was ranked #1 most livable small city in Mexico and #10 in Latin America by FDI Intelligence, a subsidiary of the Financial Times of London. I tend to agree with that august entity's assessment.

Besides agreeable climate, it's strategically located 30 miles from Pacific coast beaches, is about 50 miles from Manzanillo, and an hour and a half drive to Barra de Navidad, which has one of the nicest hotels in the region. Weekends you can be toes in the sand by the ocean, sipping on a margarita within a 40-minute drive, which is a huge positive for those who enjoy the sun and surf. It's about a two hour and change drive from Guadalajara's international airport on extremely safe toll roads which I drive regularly with no issues (other than an occasional traffic ticket due to wildly excessive speed, which is completely deserved), and because of its altitude is cooler than the coast, with steadier temperature variations regardless of the season.

Colima has a number of first-class private hospitals, as well as a public IMSS facility, and numerous veterinary clinics – important to me since I have dogs. The doctors are competent and many speak English due to their education, although many shopkeepers do not, so a little Spanish, or at least a cell phone translation app, are helpful.

The northern part of the city is the newer and better area, with the city center being typical of smaller Mexican towns, with colonial architecture and the expected churches and government edifices. It's certainly charming enough, and reminds me very much of San Miguel de Allende, with narrow winding streets and centuries old edifices. That said, I don't spend much time downtown, preferring the more attractive northern section and its more modern infrastructure and amenities, including a large mall, a second one under construction, familiar chains like WalMart, Sam's, Starbucks, McDonalds, Burger King, Pizza Hut, and all the other usual suspects. Creature comforts and consumer goods are readily available, and best of all they are as affordable as anything I've found in the decent areas of Mexico.

Colima is a seismic area, as is all of Mexico, so it gets shaken by earthquakes periodically, but rarely with any damage to modern structures (the biggest one 20 years ago destroyed many of the century old homes in the colonial downtown area, but did little to nothing to the newer buildings). It also can get hit be heavy rains when a hurricane is blowing up the coast, but because it's inland it doesn't get the high winds that make those storms so destructive, so it's really just a big rainstorm when they occasionally make landfall nearby.

You'll want a car in Colima, because it's spread out. Taxis are extremely reasonable, as in a buck or two to go pretty much anywhere, but I wouldn't want to live there permanently without a vehicle – there's too much to do that requires driving, like the beach, or the forest, or any of the nature zones outside the city limits.

Real estate is dirt cheap by any standards, with homes on the street in the northern district for $125-$225K. In the premium gated communities, they range more from $300K up to $600K or more, depending on size. There are a number of older gated neighborhoods, the notable ones being Las Parotas, Parque Royale, and Bugambilias, but they're showing their age and don't really do much for me.

The real find, in my opinion, is a five-star 18-hole golf course community seven minutes north of town, called Altozano. This is a platinum level development with a world class course, incredible clubhouse, tennis courts, restaurant and bar, pools, spa, fully equipped gym, spin classes, Pilates, yoga, the whole nine yards. It's a sprawling development that features some of the nicest amenities I've seen, with immaculate guard gated grounds, 24-hour patrols and cameras for security, high speed internet, and top shelf infrastructure at giveaway prices.

You can buy a lot and build (although most of the best lots are long gone), but that poses its own problems in Mexico, as few want to manage a construction project long distance for a year, with all the risk and angst that entails. But within the development is an expat community called El Encanto, that features a number of different single-level floorplans on larger lots, including on the fairway. The homes are designed and built to U.S. standards, and are a welcome change from the ubiquitous two-story boxy designs that typify most of the construction there – stairs are a disaster if you're older, or your knees are blown, or you're packing a few extra pounds, or you want to avoid a slip and fall that could land you in the hospital.

New homes are priced from $269K USD and up, depending on number of bedrooms and whether they're garden view or are on the fairway, and they appear to have financing in place for qualified borrowers. Full disclosure: the development is impressive enough that I bought there, and invested in El Encanto – it's the nicest area I've seen in Mexico, and the combo of single-story living on larger lots in a platinum level community at prices that harken back to the 1980's convinced me to want to reside there, as well as participate in the development's growth. Obviously I'm biased since I became an owner, just as I am in Cabo and in Zapopan, but I don't buy unless I'm really impressed, which everyone who's visited inevitably is. I know my friends are, as several who've visited wound up buying as well, reasoning that at those prices they couldn't see any reason not to.

The community has websites at ElEncantoColima.com and ElEncantoAltozano.com that are a worthwhile investment of a few minutes of one's time to get a sense of the place.

There's a story behind how I discovered Colima. I have friends who've lived in the city for generations, and I got dragged there for a wedding. Intrigued after a short visit, I went to hang out for a week for the holidays and fell in love with the town – I couldn't believe I'd never heard of it, and that none of my Mexican buddies had, either. It seemed to have everything – good restaurants, modern infrastructure, safety, creature comforts, an airport, proximity to the beach, the whole nine yards. So I began nosing around about property values to see what things cost, and was blown away by how cheap everything was, relative to Cabo, or Zapopan or Queretaro, or even Chapala or Merida.

Because my friends know my tastes, I kept being directed to check out Altozano, and when I finally drove the short distance to the grounds I couldn't believe my eyes. Here was a world class resort with amenities the developer had obviously spent a fortune on, and it was completely unknown. It had been there for a decade, it was gorgeous, the developer had other golf courses all over Mexico so was reputable and stable, the weather was perfect, the HOA dues were $150 a month (half what I paid in Vegas thirty plus years ago)…within a week I'd bought a lot on the fairway because there were no homes available for sale that were anything like what I would want to own or were built to my construction standards – the irony being that I don't even play golf (although I intend to start).

The rest, as they say, is history, and I'm an enthusiastic fan.

Outside of that development, most of the rest of the offerings are on the street, targeted to a more modest budget, both in town and in the areas at the northern tip of the city – the reason being there's virtually no crime in Colima so no real reason for most to live in gated communities, and because much of the city is composed of Mexican retirees for whom every penny saved is another available for lifestyle, so they're willing to take the security risk of a break-in that doesn't exist in gated communities.

Don't get me wrong – there's plenty of crime in Colima, *the state,* because Manzanillo is the main port on the Pacific coast and is constantly contested by various warring cartels, so the various factions kill each other left and right. And Tecoman, near the coast, is close to the border with Michoacan and plays host to La Familia Michoacana (yet another cartel), and has extremely fertile soil that is ideal for certain cash crops – so Tecoman is also often a battleground among the various warring factions. Those two make Colima *the state* one of the most dangerous per capita in the nation – largely because the entire state has something like seven hundred thousand people total, so if you see a few hundred gangsters mowed down in Manzanillo and Tecoman in a year, the per capita number is wildly high, even if the absolute number can't match a rough week in Chicago.

But Colima, the capital city, has no crime to speak of other than an occasional domestic violence call, or a political assassination of an official who took bribes from the wrong cartel. Of course, it also has the occasional burglary or petty theft, but no violent crime, which makes it hugely appealing to me, as the overall rate is lower than most places I've lived in the U.S.

One of the reasons Colima is unknown is that there's no industry in the city other than service businesses, so each younger generation moves to attend university in Guadalajara and make their fortunes elsewhere, leaving few youngsters to get into trouble. Most of the residents are older middle and upper middle-class Mexicans who either have lived there forever, or retired there, so nobody's up to no good – they've all made their money, or own businesses, and so are legitimate, not criminally inclined. There's no drug trade to speak of because there's no market in the city given the dearth of youngsters, and there's no value to it as a trafficking route, as everything moves north, up the coast, not inland.

Rents are stupid cheap. A bright, modern 3 br home in town might run $400-$600, unfurnished. A smaller home up in Altozano will cost more like $1100 per month, but you're paying for the amenities and the grounds. Most locals won't pay that much for the difference, which is why rents are so inexpensive – there are literally no expats, so they aren't there to drive the prices up.

Colima is a rare find at this point because there has been no marketing for tourism, which means that costs are as low as you can get. I expect that to change as more discover it, but for now it's a steal given what you're getting for you money.

Which brings me to prices. Beers in my favorite bar cost .80 cents. Shots run a whopping $1.75. Breakfast in most places is a couple of bucks. Lunch $3 or so. Dinner in any of the many restaurants (there are a ton at every quality level due to the number of prosperous folks living there) might cost $6-$10 in one of the better places. For whatever reason there are dozens of hand-crafted pizza restaurants, in addition to all the usual chains, like Pizza Hut, Little Caesar's, Domino's. Every other corner has a convenience store – either an Oxxo, or a Kiosko (like a 7-11, with the entire chain also owned by the Altozano developer), where items like beer are .50 cents, as a frame of reference. A visit to the ER is $30, a doctor's visit more like $20. I could go on for hours. Medicine is about a fifth of the cost in the U.S. I was asked by a friend to look up her blood pressure medicine she has a $55 co-pay for in the States, and it is $11 for the same dosage and quantity in any pharmacy. A maid might cost $3 an hour for 4 hours. $250 full time. A car wash is $2.00. A qualified mechanic charges $7-$10 an hour.

In Colima, if you own your own house, a couple could live like royalty on their social security of between $1500-$1800 a month. Not just get by, but live on the golf course, eat out most meals, have a maid and a gardener as often as they wish, play tennis or lounge by the pool or get a massage, visit the doctor or dentist, cover their meds…and still have money left over at month's end. To me that's incredible. The only other area I've found where that's possible in safety and with contemporary infrastructure and amenities is Merida, but I just can't deal with the weather (or the AC bills – in Colima, you only need AC a few months out of the year, so you aren't getting whacked by thousands of dollars of electric every year like Merida). And Merida's golf course homes are more expensive – about $100K more for an equivalent place, although there aren't really any single level floorplans I could find, and that's a deal killer for many retirees who are getting up there in age. If $20K annual budget would be a nice life in Colima, for $32K a couple would be rolling Vegas style, at a level of luxury that it would take $150K+ back in the old country to live.

Colima is naturally beautiful, and has a host of outdoor activities for the so inclined. It also has a bevy of nearby interests, including forest trails and hiking, mountain biking, four wheeling. If golf or tennis or swimming are your thing, Altozano has that covered. And there's a pair of volcanoes about 20 miles north of the city, at the border of Jalisco and Colima state that are picturesque and feature very good rustic restaurants for brunch. One of the volcanoes is active, but the city is well out of range and has never suffered any damage from its infrequent eruptions – if you've studied geography you'll know that this type of volcano's danger zone extends no more than 3 miles from the cone, and at 5 miles the risk drops to moderate. Past that there's no risk, other than the nuisance of occasional ash from it puffing into the sky. But it makes for an amazing skyline, which reminds me somewhat of the iconic Fuji in Japan.

Some friends of mine are opening an Italian restaurant and an Argentine steak house in Colima soon, which proves that for the entrepreneurial, there are plenty of options. One had the top steak place in Cabo for years, and another a hugely popular Italian place, and both want to establish a foothold in town. Since their concepts did well in the most competitive market in Mexico (Cabo has something like 280 restaurants in a postage stamp size area), they figure it will be a slam dunk in Colima, which is larger and has an enthusiastic local restaurant crowd. I can think of a dozen other business opportunities that would do well, but I don't have the hours in the day – the point being there's a lot of promise in this quiet little hamlet.

Colima also boasts the #2 rated hotel in all of Mexico (Conde Nast) – the Hacienda De San Antonio, which has played host for all manner of celebrities and European royalty (UK celebrity and corporate raider Jimmy Goldsmith owned it). Pretty impressive considering that the Four Seasons, Ritz Carlton, and a bevy of others were also in the running.

Colima has an airport with national flights, but to reach it without connections it's easier to fly into either Guadalajara, or Manzanillo. I've done both, and I prefer Guadalajara because of the large number of options to the States, as well as all of mainland and Baja.

In summary, Colima represents the best of the places I've highlighted due to safety, price, amenities, livable weather, and lifestyle. If golf course living in a luxury resort are your thing, look no further, because you won't find anything close – and believe me, I've looked, in addition to having built dozens of seriously high-end custom homes on the best golf courses in Baja. If you're trying to maximize your value and live like a celebrity on a modest budget in premium style, I've yet to find anything that can beat it, so anyone considering relocating would be well advised to add it to their short list.

- Affordability: 5 stars
- Climate: 4.25 stars
- Safety: 5 stars
- Healthcare: 5 stars
- Technology accessibility: 5 stars
- Accessibility (Time to get to a major U.S. city): San Diego, 3 hr flight, Dallas and Arizona, 2 hours and change from Guadalajara airport
- High temperature in Summer: 85 F
- Low temperature in Winter: 64 F at night
- Average daily temp 75-80 F year-round.

Photos of Colima:
tripadvisor.com/Attractions-g153983-Activities-Colima_Pacific_Coast.html

Photos of El Encanto and Altozano:
https://www.altozano-colima.com/en/

For an excellent resource on cost comparisons between where you live now, and your target destination in Mexico, this website is invaluable: numbeo.com/cost-of-living/compare_countries_result.jsp?country1=Mexico&country2=United+States

Chapter 3

–

Visas, Taxes, Sales Tax and Licenses

Now that you're familiar with the venues I recommend, you'll need to come up to speed on the permits you'll need to live in Mexico, as well as understand the various taxes you'll encounter.

Tourist Visa

Most tourists enter and leave Mexico using a tourist card. This is a temporary visa allowing you free access to any part of Mexico. If you fly in, it's taken care of by the airline (handed out on the plane) and the cost is included by the airline. The card, called the Visitante, is valid for up to six months (a hundred-eighty days) with multiple entries. Make sure you ask for the full 180 days even if you plan a short stay – if you decide to return in that hundred-eighty days you just saved yourself $25.

According to the law you need the tourist card with you at all times when traveling. You'll need a current passport in order to get one.

Immigration offices won't accept money for the card (theoretically), so you need to go to a bank to get the card stamped as paid; then you'll need to go back to Immigration, or the next Immigration office in the next town you visit, and they'll need to stamp it as valid. Reality is that you won't need one for any reason other than to leave by plane. I've never had mine checked other than at the airport flying north to the States, and frankly, a few times I lost the damn thing, and wound up having to pay a $35 to $50 fee to Immigration at the airport in order for them to issue a new one, which they were happy to do. When I do that it's unclear how much if any of that fee goes to the official coffers, however I'm typically not that concerned about it, especially if I've been in-country for nine months instead of two or three. Generally, I'll explain that I drove down and lost my card, and that's the only explanation required, along with the fee. Seems fair to me.

One caution if you're driving – there are military checkpoints set up every hundred-fifty miles or so, manned by teenage soldiers with M16's. They're there as part of a cooperation agreement with the U.S. to stop the flow of drugs to the border – something they've been conspicuously poor at doing judging by the size of the narcotics business in the States. They generally will just wave you through headed south, but will do an inspection when you travel north, sometimes extending to going through your luggage and searching the entire car, including the underside and fenders.

A common question is what happens if you stay in Mexico on your tourist card after it expires? The short answer in general is, nothing, unless you try to get a job or start a business or do any sort of work. I know the rules say you aren't supposed to stay without getting a temporary residence card or a permanent residence card, but reality is that many do, for years, and nothing happens. Realistically, though, you should get either a temp or permanent card if you're going to stick around, however there's no mechanism in place to force you to get one, or that will check to see whether you have one.

Note that I'm not suggesting anyone flout the immigration rules, but rather just addressing a topic that comes up regularly. One caveat is that if you need to fly back to the States or Canada, you'll need to give the airline ticket person your tourist card. As previously described, if you "lost" it you'll be directed to go to the Immigration office at the airport, where you can secure another one for the aforementioned fee, which again seems to vary depending upon the mood of whoever is working. You then need to bring that new card back to the airline, who only then will issue a boarding pass. Hint: No amount of complaining or excuses will get the airline to let you on board without tendering a tourist card, so save your energy.

Residence Cards

If you've decided to live or retire in Mexico, you'll need a permanent or temporary residence visa to do so legally. I would tend to recommend going for the permanent as a retiree if you aren't planning to work and are fifty or older, or as one of the many types of vocational visas if you do intend to work. As with many things in Mexico, the procedures and rules tend to change for no apparent reason, so while what follows is current as of the date of this editing, you'd be best advised to go to the Mexican immigration website to verify the latest rules and processes. That Web address is www.inm.gob.mx/EN/index.php

As of this writing, those wishing to obtain temporary residence as a retiree need to show at least $1950 USD monthly income from non-Mexican sources over the last half year, or $32,400 (roughly) in savings for at least one year, with bank statements for six months. Those wishing to obtain permanent residency will need to demonstrate at least $3250 per month for the last six months, or at least $130,000 in savings over the last year, with bank statements. Married couples need to add $650 per month to the above numbers for the spouse.

Temporary Resident Visa

This is the one-size-fits-all visa, and it's good for a year, at the end of which it will need to be renewed annually for up to four years. You can get one at any Mexican Consulate (if you're not in Mexico yet), or rather, you can get a sticker for your passport that will enable you to pick up your card once in Mexico – but you have to go to Immigration within 30 days of arrival to do so. There are several types of these visas, including Lucrative, if you plan to work, or Non-Lucrative, if you don't. The various criteria, including the amount of savings or monthly income you'll need to be able to prove you have, in order to get one, can be easily found online, and because they can change periodically I haven't listed them here. I would encourage you to do your research for how these are being handled now, as there is no guarantee that today's procedure is anything like yesterday's.

Permanent Resident Visa

This visa is intended for those seeking permanent resident status in Mexico, including those who intend to eventually seek Mexican Citizenship.

To be granted one, you need to prove you have sufficient income to support yourself or have substantial assets, or have close family connections in Mexico, or have 4 consecutive years of temporary residency visa (or 2 years of it if you married a Mexican citizen), or be a political refugee. There are a few other criteria that apply, but again, these can change, including a points system, and you'd do best checking the process online.

When your permanent residence visa has been issued, you're entitled to the full rights (like access to IMSS sick pay) and responsibilities (like paying income tax on Mexican income) as any other Mexican citizen, with the exception of the right to vote. Foreigners are not allowed to involve themselves in "internal Mexican affairs" and can't hold public office.

Once your full residence status has been accepted you can also begin your application for Mexican citizenship, although you don't have to; you can remain a 'resident alien' on a permanent residence card with no ill effects.

Your permanent residence card will enable you to pass through Mexico's borders as if you were a Mexican National.

You do not, under Mexican law, need to surrender your national passport -- whether you remain a resident-alien or apply for citizenship -- which you can use when you return to your home country: either for visits, or when returning home permanently.

I would advise anyone considering navigating the waters of temporary or permanent residence visas to contact an immigration consultant, or attorney, to lubricate the way and ensure you are successful in your application. For a small cost you can eliminate a lot of headaches, and this is not something you want to get wrong.

CURP

Permanent residents will need to secure a Clave Unica Registro Poblacion (CURP) number, which is an 18-character long national identification number used to identify all residents of Mexico, as well as all Mexican citizens living abroad. It can be obtained by visiting your local Registry Civil office or when opening a bank account, where you will be required to provide a passport and your temp or permanent resident visa as proof of residence, along with a copy of each. I like the information page that can be found at curp.troyaestrategias.com, which explains all about the CURP and how to get one. Or for a listing of Registry Civil offices so you can find the closest one to you, go to http://www.tramitanet.gob.mx/index.html and then select "Consulta de la CURP," and then select the last link, "Oficina de atencion CURP." A list will be displayed, and you can choose whichever state you're in from there.

Income Tax

If you earn income in Mexico, you will owe Mexican income tax, which is on a sliding scale up to a max of 35%. If you do not earn income in Mexico, you owe no income tax, unless you are a permanent resident, in which case, you would owe that tax on your worldwide income (subject to dual taxation treaties) if you have a "lucrativo" status (meaning you can work in Mexico), but not if you are "retirement" status unable to legally work in Mexico – where any income from abroad is treated as retirement income not subject to tax in Mexico.

From a practical standpoint, Mexico has no mechanism to learn what you've earned elsewhere, just as the U.S. had no mechanism before it forced the world to adopt FACTA reporting or be barred from the dollar-based SWIFT network. If you want a more definitive answer, however, I would suggest you speak with a Mexican accountant who can clarify how the rules are enforced so you have a better understanding of what is due, and what you are required to report. Rules change, and you don't want to make assumptions when it comes to which type of permanent residence to apply for. Note that if you become a Mexican citizen after the statutory waiting period and get a passport, you will owe tax on your worldwide income.

If you are a U.S. citizen, you would have to file a return if you earned more than $24K per year, however if the income was earned outside the U.S., you would pay no tax on the first $107,600.00 earned, per person. However, the U.S. rules are byzantine and complex, so you would be well advised to speak with an American accountant in order to understand your actual burden, if any, and what is excluded from tax. I won't go into ways to structure your affairs so you aren't subject to tax anywhere – that would be the topic for a completely different book. But trust me that it can be done, perfectly legally, just as WalMart, Apple, IBM, Starbucks, Carnival, and just about every major corporation has been doing for years.

For capital gains taxes, any profit you generate buying low and selling high in Mexico would theoretically be subject to cap gains treatment, but that really only becomes an issue when buying and selling property, at which point you would be well advised to contact an accountant or tax attorney in Mexico to understand your options and anything owed. It is beyond the scope of this book to offer a comprehensive treatment of the intricacies of those taxes and the mechanisms and exclusions to reduce any tax owed, so talk to a professional if this is of interest. That said, if you have permanent resident status, you can qualify for an exemption on cap gains tax on the sale of your primary residence in Mexico every five years. A Mexican accountant or tax attorney would be able to address this exemption for you.

Property Tax

Property taxes in Mexico are laughably low, and that shows no signs of changing anytime soon. As an example, I pay a few hundred dollars a year for each of my homes, which are in the five thousand sq. foot range. In the U.S., that would be tens of thousands of dollars. But not in Mexico.

Property taxes vary depending upon the area, as some areas are zoned as rural (most of them, actually) and have even lower taxes than I pay in one of the more expensive areas. I have a beachfront lot a few miles outside of Cabo where I think I pay $25 a year for a quarter acre plot of land. You'll find that property taxes are a non-issue for the most part, and will shake your head in amazement the first year you get a bill.

Sales Tax

Mexico currently has a sixteen percent sales tax (IVA – a value added tax) on all purchases except food and mortgage insurance. Restaurant meals are subject to tax, however prices include IVA, as do prices in many large stores. It's just easier for the consumer to understand the final selling price than having to try to calculate IVA, so places like Costco and WalMart roll it into the published price.

Licenses

If you decide to live in Mexico you'll probably want to get a Mexican driver's license if you plan to drive much. The law actually dictates that if you have a temp or permanent residence card you have to have a Mexican license, and are restricted from driving cars with non-Mexican plates.

Getting a Mexican license is relatively simple. You go to the municipal headquarters, fill out a bunch of paperwork, pay $40 USD or so (it changes regularly), get your photo taken, and presto, there's your license. Alternatively, in some expat friendly areas you can go to one of the "facilitator" companies that specialize in handling all official paperwork for Gringos, and they will handle most of it, and escort you to the office at the appropriate time to get your photo taken and pick up your license.

I recommend you use the facilitators, unless you have infinite patience and time, and speak relatively fluent Spanish. Virtually nobody in an official position at the municipal headquarters is going to admit to speaking English, so you're on your own unless you use a middleman. That's why there are numerous of these types of groups around in Baja and some of the areas I've mentioned – there's strong demand for someone who will make all the bureaucracy go away and just get you what you want in the most efficient manner possible. I've found it's worth the money to have someone deal with things like immigration and licenses – having spent many months and dozens of visits to official offices trying to get an item that a facilitator was able to get me in two weeks and one visit, I can speak to this first hand. Don't be a cheapskate when it comes to your immigration status or getting things like licenses or permits.

The only other type of license you're likely to ever encounter while living in Mexico is a building permit, if you decide to do construction. Building permits will generally be handled by your contractor, and you'll virtually never get involved in obtaining one. So rather than devoting a section on a type of license you're never going to have to secure yourself, I'll simply say that for any construction or additions, hire a reputable, knowledgeable professional with a good track record and strong recent references, and he'll deal with the inevitable paperwork for you.

Chapter 4

–

Real Estate – Renting, Owning, Building, Mortgages, Home Insurance

Rentals

Once you've researched the various areas and decided on which of the numerous alternatives best fit your lifestyle and overall requirements, you'll have to tackle the nuts and bolts of finding a place to live. Most will choose to rent for some period before they buy, which isn't a bad call.

Most rentals in Baja come furnished, so furniture poses no problem for moving in. This is because it's expensive to import things from abroad, so anyone who wants a shot at getting a renter has to do so furnished. There are exceptions at the lower level of the market, but they are exceptions, not the rule. On mainland, most rentals will be unfurnished, however I've found furnished places in every area I mention in this books, so it's not impossible, just more time consuming.

When you're scoping out areas to rent, I'd advise you to talk to the local real estate people, and find out if there's someone who specializes in long-term rentals. Those listings will be a bit pricier than renting directly from the owner, but you'll have a better idea of what you're getting into, assuming the agent is reputable. Too often I've seen folks spot an ad in the local supermarket for a condo or home for rent, and get themselves into ugly situations. Typical is an inexpensive home that appears to be in good shape, but is actually in an area with poor or no security, and thus a target of opportunity for petty theft and car break-ins. Or you rent a bargain, only to find that the wiring is intermittent, the plumbing disastrous, and the landlord incommunicado when it comes time to fix problems (but not to collect the rent – they're always there for rent collection).

Having said that, some communities offer pretty good networking for rentals, either on the Internet or via local publications. In the Cabo and San Jose area, the Gringo Gazette publishes classified ads that feature good rental exposure. In the East Cape area of Los Barriles, there are a number of online bulletin boards where Gringos advertise rentals. On mainland, Inmuebles24.com is a good resource, as is Trovit.com.mx, but to a lesser extent. Later, in chapter 8, you'll find listed a host of Web resources you can use to do research, so don't worry about exact addresses right now. Just understand that the Web has rapidly become the medium of choice for the rental market in many areas, so if you aren't highly Internet savvy, you might want to start practicing. There's a wealth of info out there, as well as a ton of community-oriented stuff like weather, local scuttlebutt, news on new businesses, etc. so you'd be foolish not to avail yourself of it.

As far as prices go, it will depend on which area you look, and what amenities you want. I've seen modest one-bedroom apartments in marginal neighborhoods go for a few hundred dollars a month, and I've also seen seven-thousand-foot dream homes renting for $5K and up. My advice is to spend a few hours online studying the offerings in whatever area you're thinking about, and you'll quickly get a feel for prices.

Most rentals will want references of some sort, as well as first month's rent and a security deposit. Rarely will you get offered a written agreement, but it's in your best interests to insist on one – that is in Spanish as well as in English. Contracts in English aren't legal in Mexico, so you have to get the Spanish language version, and if necessary use an online translator to ensure that the terms are as agreed. While it isn't uncommon to rent without a written agreement, it's a recipe for disaster when it comes time for deposit returns, and repairs. So get it in writing, being friendly but firm in the request.

One important note. Mexico is the land of *manana,* so you should require anyplace you rent to be cleaned before you move in, as well as any repairs completed before you accept occupancy. If you hear stories about how the place is GOING to be painted, or cleaned, or fixed up before you take possession, just assume none of that will happen. Come up with a compromise where you sign a deal contingent on it being done before you put up any money, or chances are you'll be disappointed with what you wind up with.

Take photos with a digital camera of all furniture and any noted deficiencies before or when you move in, using the date function to memorialize when the photos were taken. That will come in handy on move-out if your landlord insists that the broken chair in the dining room or the missing tile in the kitchen is your fault. There's nothing like a photographic record for keeping everyone honest.

On a final note, oftentimes you won't see your security deposit back, no matter how good a tenant you've been, as the landlord probably spent it. The best way to handle that is when you know you're going to move, contact the landlord a month before, and do a tour of the property. Get him to agree as to condition, and if he can't give you the deposit back then, be sympathetic but also negotiate reducing the last month's rent by eighty percent of the amount held as security deposit. That way you won't leave too much on the table when you move on. Oh, and if a landlord wants first, last, and security deposit, I'd look elsewhere, as you've lost your leverage on getting your security deposit back (unless it's really nominal). Not to say don't do the deal, but you shouldn't have too much as a security deposit if you've paid first and last or you risk never seeing that money again. Caveat Emptor.

If there's a dispute, forget about the Mexican court system. There's no such thing as small claims court, and you'll pay ten times whatever the disputed amount is on attorneys, so just leave it out of your thinking.

Buying

Many Gringos wind up buying once they've been in Mexico for a while or they've really researched it, and for good reason. Land is relatively cheap, and prices are generally far, far lower than the U.S.

When buying, there's one rule you need to remember. A property isn't worth what it was yesterday, or what the seller hopes it will be worth tomorrow; it's worth whatever someone is willing to pay today. Tomorrow's values are hopes, and yesterday's are memories. Understanding that, you also need to realize there's an intrinsic value to everything, and if you try to be too brutal on your negotiations, even in a buyer's market you're likely to have the seller walk away. You'll also run into something called "reverse capital gains," where if you buy for less than the value the property is manifested for, you'll owe tax as though you had earned capital gains on the difference between that price and your purchase price. There are some creative ways around that, but best to understand what you're doing or you could get a nasty surprise at the close when it's too late to back out or renegotiate – it isn't the seller's responsibility to educate you about possible tax issues you incur by being aggressive on your buy price.

Get a good real estate agent who knows the area and is conscientious, and who's interested in making sure you get the best value for your dollar, not just in making the fastest sale. I was fortunate enough to have a great one when I went shopping for land in Cabo, and she advised me against a few "opportunities" that I'm now glad she counseled against. There's no substitute for someone who's been around for a decade or two and knows the ropes, as well as the stories on all the developments and neighborhoods. In the long run, it's the only way to go.

Property in Baja and coastal areas of mainland is bought and sold using a "Fideicomiso," which is a land trust. The reason a Fideicomiso is used is that all Baja and coastal areas are designated as areas that are restricted from foreign ownership. To solve this legal obstacle, the Fideicomiso was created, wherein a bank (Mexican) owns the property (thus no foreign ownership issues) but lets you, the Fideicomiso beneficiary, use or sell the land as you like. It's a lawyerly way to get around the prohibitions against foreign ownership, and it's one hundred percent safe and effective. Unless you're a Mexican citizen, you'll be buying and selling property via Fideicomisos. Ask your real estate agent for all the details.

On mainland, if you're not on the coast you won't face those issues, and you can simply own the property outright, just like back home. Long gone are the days where you had to lease the land beneath your house, which was a clumsy way of circumventing the prohibition against foreigners owning coastal land that died out when the Fideicomiso came into being.

You'll also need to vet any offering to ensure there's clear title, and that the seller actually has the right to sell it, and that it's free of any encumbrances. A good real estate agent can also help with that. Just understand there aren't nearly the legal protections you would have in the U.S., so you have to be on your guard against anything that seems odd or doesn't pass the sniff test. Seasoned real estate professionals spend a lot of their time researching listings to protect their clients, so this is an area they need to be adept and experienced in. Your buyer's broker is your only real defense against disaster or duplicity. You don't really require this protection in the large, reputable developments that have in-house sales teams, however it's absolutely mandatory that you get verification of clear title elsewhere before you plunk down cash.

The internet is awash in horror stories of Gringos having

their properties "stolen" by crooked locals, either through squatting, or failing to respect property rights, or by illegally forging titles. My advice is that if you stick to established areas in communities where title is clear, you won't have issues. All of the stories I'm aware of involved someone buying land in an unincorporated area, usually rural or beachfront in some desolate area, and then learning that there is a dispute of some sort. It is for this reason that all of my investments, including my beachfront land in Cabo, are in reputable developments. I've built homes for a number of high net worth foreigners in remote reaches where they've learned there is disagreement about the provenance of the title – a la "my grandfather lost it in a card game, but he was cheated" or "they registered it as theirs even though my dad was never paid in full." The threat here is obviously that your property will be held up for years in litigation, and the gambit is for you to pay to make it go away. If you stick to the mainstream areas and developments, this won't be an issue, which is why I don't roll the dice on bargains in deserted locales.

Once you've decided to buy, the question is really what sort of property matches your lifestyle, as well as your likely lifestyle a decade or two out. A condo? Raw land? A house? A house in a guard-gated community? Most areas offer all the above, so think long and hard about not just what you'll be happy with today, but what you'll require five and ten years from now. A condo with a flight or two of stairs may seem like a dream when you're fifty-five, but at seventy years old, could be a deathtrap. A cozy small home may be claustrophobic in a few years. A seemingly safe neighborhood may be poised for decline, if you only knew the signs to look for.

Rule number one of buying in Mexico (after verifying title) is to know your exit. What I mean is that in many areas there isn't a ton of liquidity at any given time, so it can take years to sell a property unless it's very desirable or fire-sale priced. When you're a buyer, put yourself in the shoes of being a seller in a few years, and just assume the market is difficult. What price will you need to offer your place for to get out relatively quickly? If your buying price doesn't match up with your most pessimistic take on future selling price, then you're paying too much, or at least too much for your own good. Be pragmatic about buying, and don't fall in love.

Condos are by far the most popular choice for retirees and expats, largely because of affordability and convenience. The positives are obvious – low entry price, shared expenses on landscaping, etc. The negatives are not as immediately obvious – problematic homeowners' associations, annoying neighbors, noise along shared walls, steadily increasing dues, low appreciation relative to stand-alone homes. But for many, balancing it all out, a condo's the preferred choice, and Mexico has plenty of them.

The next level up is the developer-built stand-alone home communities, which generally have 1700 to 2000 sq. foot dwellings placed close together, but with no shared walls. These are usually also relatively affordable, however vary greatly by how dependable the developer ultimately is. There are many communities that have disastrous construction, sewage treatment, plumbing, electric, etc. because the developer failed to live up to even the most minimal promises, so again, it's best to have an agent who knows the ropes to keep you from getting burned by selecting one of these. Nobody advertises "Nightmare for sale", so you have to be skeptical when shopping.

The next level up is the guard-gated community, either developer built, or sold as lots and built by the individual lot owners. These are usually at the higher end of the price curve, as you have twenty-four-hour security, and full custom homes where care was presumably taken in the construction process. Obvious good information to know going in is what percentage of the community is paid current on its dues (if many aren't paying, who's going to continue subsidizing the security and amenities you're considering buying into?), and what disputes or lawsuits are taking place with the HOA or between owners. You can choose many things, but you don't always get to choose your neighbors, so it's a good idea to get a feel for the community gestalt before making a buying decision.

Finally, there's raw land, either in a subdivision or just out there somewhere. Subdivisions offer a level of protection in terms of CC&Rs, infrastructure, and clear title, and are generally the best way to go. As I said before, raw land in undeveloped areas has inherent title risks, as there are often disputes on who really owns what. Often, these can pop up years after you buy. The only counsel I can give you on this is absolutely, positively, always buy title insurance if you buy land that isn't in a subdivision. To not do so is suicide. I can recount story after story of purchases where title insurance "wasn't needed" that have turned into decade long lawsuits, rendering the land unsellable.

If you buy raw land, make sure you first do your homework on building costs, as you may find you can't actually build that dream house you believed you could for anywhere near what you guessed. Construction costs have roughly doubled since 2010, and show no signs of coming down, so don't just assume you can work a miracle and build at 2010 prices. Wages increase about six percent on average per year (as do material costs) so run the numbers on labor costs over a decade and that piece of the puzzle will start to make sense. And finally, many of the materials used in better homes are imported, so taxes and tariffs and such come into play. Add it all together and it quickly becomes obvious why you have to be careful in your assumptions.

However you decide to go, the process is the same: you'll have to go to a notary, pay whatever the acquisition tax is (varies by state, but usually 2-3% of the sales price), and sign a ream of documents. Closing can take months, so patience is a virtue. In Mexico, a notary isn't a store owner with a stamp, it's an attorney who has the additional power of a judge, so notary fees won't be as nominal as back home. Ask for an estimate of closing costs so you don't get blindsided.

Building

Building a custom home is problematic in even the most developed countries, so it should come as no surprise that it can be difficult in Mexico as well. Perhaps more so than elsewhere, as there are no building inspectors, and the building code is loose, to put it mildly. Add into the mix that there's a fair share of larcenous operators as well as incompetents building, and it can seem like a daunting task.

Horror stories abound, and for good reason. If you're going to build here, unless it's a reputable firm or developer, you really need to be on top of every phase of construction, and you really are only as good as your contractor is honest. One obvious and easy way of protecting yourself is to check references on whoever you're considering, and to really look hard at their recent work. Many builders have fallen on hard times, and are cutting corners to get the low bid. Others will simply lie, and go in with an absurdly low bid they know they can't honor, figuring they'll move you up once you're pregnant and the project is well underway. Still others use inferior labor, or junk materials, or black-market steel, or shoddy plumbing and electric, all to put more money into their pocket.

There are many honorable, competent builders in Mexico, but there are also plenty of snakes and flim-flam men. Quite a few are either playing out of their league but want the work, or simply aren't qualified to build a home but don't want to admit it. Still others are drunks, or crooks, or hacks – and none will tell you, thus it's up to you to figure it out.

I would recommend to anyone considering building in Mexico to get a copy of my book on the topic (yes, I actually wrote the book on construction in Mexico), written under the name C. Phil Osso, titled "This 'Ol Casa – Building in Baja 101", available from Amazon and Barnes and Noble https://www.amazon.com/This-Ol-Casa-Building-Laymans/dp/1440126755. It was written as a primer for novices planning to build for the first time, and catalogs all the ways you can get screwed, as well as precautions to ensure you don't. There simply is no other book or guide like it available, and I know plenty of people who have read it and saved themselves a lot of heartache. The only other book I've ever seen mentioned regarding the Mexican construction experience is *God and Mr. Gomez,* which was written before the personal computer was invented, and is an amusing read but offers exactly zero practical advice. Again, if you're entertaining the notion of building a home in Mexico, get the book, as it will save you thousands of times its purchase price in avoided catastrophes and disasters. That's my shameless plug, but you'll thank me once you've read it.

Now, lest all these warnings scare you away from considering building, let me also say you can build homes here at quality levels undreamt of in the U.S. for far less than you could build equivalently constructed homes for there. The main reason is that labor is a fraction of what it is up North, which is why homes in Mexico can be built out of materials that last centuries and don't blow away every time there's a hurricane (can you say Florida, anyone?) or rot to pieces in a marine environment (anyone who's ever dealt with a wood frame and sheetrock structure in the States near the coast knows exactly what I'm talking about).

You just need to be careful, pragmatic, and do your homework. You can wing it if you like, but Mexico is littered with the bodies of Gringos who thought they were going to show the locals how it's done. I'm here to tell you that, as with purchasing, you need the most competent protection you can get, as there isn't any building department or other official who's going to come out and make sure your house isn't a disaster. You're only as good as your contractor is, so you need to arm yourself with as much info as possible before you embark on this course.

I've personally built dozens of homes in Baja and on

mainland, ranging from mid-quality spec homes to full blown luxury mansions on beaches, and I can tell you that building here is as tough as it is anywhere. But I can also say that some of the nicest homes in Mexico are in Baja, so done correctly the outcome can be rewarding from both a quality as well as an economic perspective.

It's beyond the scope of this book to offer reams of information on building in Mexico, so I hope you follow my advice and get, "This "Ol Casa", or else are extremely lucky. Those are the only two ways I know that can guarantee a positive outcome on a building project here.

Mortgages

Most property in Mexico is bought using cash. Many folks pull equity from their U.S. or Canadian residences using refinancing or second mortgages, and "finance" their purchases that way – but getting a loan in Mexico is currently difficult, if not impossible, for Gringos. In the mid-2000's, U.S. style funding came into some areas of Mexico big time, and it partially drove a jump in property values, as suddenly you didn't actually have to have the money to buy that dream home – you could borrow it. That was great while it lasted, but then the economy fell out of bed in 2008, and the same aggressive lenders who were offering U.S.-style mortgages disappeared. The risk adversity that the economic crises caused made even the largest, most stable lenders pull in their horns and rethink mortgage lending in Mexico.

Generally speaking, the best way to buy property is to have

your money lined up before entering into the negotiation, because if you haven't actually got the cash in the bank, the whole transaction comes into question. The moment the seller's broker hears the answer to the question, "Are you planning to finance this" in the affirmative, your perceived ability to perform drops by ninety percent. Perhaps things will change again, as they have before, but as of now that's how the landscape looks.

Some Mexican banks will do mortgages for permanent residents, but interest rates are high, in the 8-12% range or more, and qualifying can be an endurance test, as every bank seems to have its own unique set of requirements, some of which include a credit score in Mexico that you can only obtain if you're employed and have Mexican credit cards. Rather than attempting to write fifty pages on the various qualifications, I would advise you to research your Mexican bank's criteria if this is something you hope to avail yourself of. And ultimately, I would advise you not to count on it, as it can be a mercurial process with no guarantees.

There are also groups that will write a mortgage for credit-worthy U.S. citizens at 40% down, but there are no deals, and they'll generally charge 3% as a doc fee, and their rates will be anywhere from 8-12%. One such example is www.GlobalMortgage.mx – I would strongly advise getting pre-qualified if this is of interest, as you won't be taken seriously if you haven't got a loan approved when you make an offer, and many sellers won't give you the time of day. As of this writing, there are no construction loans I know of in Mexico for non-Mexican citizens, but as with most things south of the border, that is subject to change.

Finally, there is always a hybrid approach where you negotiate with the seller for them to carry a portion of the sale for a few years at a mutually agreed upon interest rate. When I've done this, it's been at 6-7% for three years, and I've never had a problem, however as with most things, your mileage may vary, and you'd be well advised to speak to an attorney or real estate specialist to ensure you don't get screwed.

Home Insurance

One question that often arises is about the availability of homeowner's insurance in Mexico, and whether it's a good idea or not. The answer is yes, there are a number of companies writing policies in Mexico, and the rates are relatively reasonable. But as with many things here, there's a catch to the, "Is it a good idea?" question.

In Mexico, ninety-eight percent of construction is out of cement block or brick, and rebar, and maybe two percent is out of 3D Styrofoam panel coated with several inches of concrete – effectively as strong and resistant as block and rebar. So fires aren't an issue – one of the main sources of destruction of homes in the U.S., and one of the reasons premiums are much higher there, is wood frame homes with sheetrock tend to light like a match. Concrete doesn't burn, so fire's off the table in terms of risk.

The biggest risk to a home in Baja and Yucatan is the unpredictable but sometimes extreme storm season – hurricanes hit with some regularity in Southern Baja (Northern tends to get spared due to the cooler water temperature – hurricanes require warm water to gather and maintain energy). Water damage from hurricanes is the number one cause of destruction in Southern Baja.

The problem is that every homeowner's insurance policy I've seen excludes damage from hurricanes, unless you have hurricane shutters or other protection installed – an investment of tens of thousands of dollars. My issue with this is that once you've spent all the money on the protection, you're protected, so the insurance isn't really such a great bet. It is if you're the insurance company, obviously, as you're collecting nice premiums to cover a home from something it's already completely protected from, however I'm not so sure it's a smart investment from a homeowner's perspective.

Let's assume you're paying $5K a year to protect your million-dollar home, but there is a fairly decent deductible of a few grand, and you've had to spend $20K on hurricane screens for all the glass in the home. Assuming something happens (other than constant sun, the only thing that is going to happen will be a hurricane, or an earthquake), you'll have to sustain at least $7 to $8K of damage for the policy to have been a good bet. If you've had the policy for two years, you have to factor two years of premiums ($10K total) plus the deductible of $2 or $3K, meaning that in order for it to be a good deal you need to have sustained $12K to $13K of damage (which implies that the insurance company will pay off hundred cent dollars – after Odile in 2014, many big companies simply said we're paying fifty cents on the dollar, or we'll declare bankruptcy and you'll get nothing. True story. Obviously everyone took the reduced payout).

So what about earthquakes? With block and rebar construction, even if the home gets riddled with cracks from an earthquake, you pay a couple of guys a grand or less to patch and paint all of them, and that's it. So not such a good deal there on the insurance, as the repair cost doesn't even burn the deductible. You'll still have to pay, because it's below the insurance deductible threshold. If a hurricane hits, maybe you have some water damage from a faulty roof. Again, figure a few grand to fix the plaster, and paint, and redo the roof waterproofing. Still not such a great idea to have insurance for that. Or say a pipe bursts. You call a plumber, he comes out and cuts a hole in the wall, fixes the leak, and then puts mortar and plaster over the hole, and paints it. Probably well under a grand.

The truth is there are very few instances where you're going to have many thousands of dollars of problems with your home that aren't excluded in the rider. Which is why insurance is so much cheaper in Mexico. The companies know you'll basically hardly ever use it, thus it isn't much of a risk for them to write the policy.

My philosophy, having lived here for 16 years, is that preventive maintenance is the best insurance. Waterproofing your roof, redoing silicone seals around windows, clearing drains, sealing your flooring, all done annually, are the best insurance you can have. There is a cost to owning a home, and I've found that budgeting a couple hundred dollars every few months for minor repairs and wear and tear is reasonable – and if you haven't paid for any maintenance for a few years, all you've done is defer it, as there will come a day of reckoning when you'll need to have the repairs done and they will be far more costly as entropy has its way with your house than if you had taken care of things in a timely manner. Having said that, if it makes you sleep better at night, then by all means get some insurance. It can't hurt. But the good news is that it isn't all that necessary, as far as I can see. Look at some pricing and policies, read the exclusions and all the fine print carefully, and then use your best judgment as to how to proceed.

Chapter 5

–

Banking, Currency, Social Security, and Automobile Ownership, Insurance & Advice

Banking

Virtually every developed area in Mexico has one or more bank branches. Anything with a population even in the low four digits will likely have several branches, along with ATMs in strategic locations. Larger metropolitan areas will have as many bank branches as anywhere in North America, so the good news is you're never far from a bank.

All banks in Baja offer dollar accounts and peso accounts. Obviously, it being Mexico, the peso is the official currency, however in most tourist areas dollars are used interchangeably. But you'll usually get taken to the cleaners on the exchange rate anywhere but at the bank, so when you live here you're best off having both a dollar and a peso account, and converting your monthly bills and spending money into pesos when the exchange rate is favorable. Numerous websites offer interbank rates on currency exchange. I use Intercam Banco in San Jose del Cabo, and usually get less than 10 basis points off interbank from them on conversions over a few grand. Other banks charge as much as 100 basis points, so it's wise to shop around and not just assume that you're getting a fair rate.

Banks on mainland won't offer dollar accounts because they

aren't in what is considered border enterprise zones, and thus there's no good reason for dollars to be used with any regularity. So if you're looking at mainland, get used to the idea that your dollar account will remain in the US or Canada, and you'll be converting to pesos for your monthly burn – not that bad once you get used to it.

Banks in Mexico operate a bit differently than in the U.S. in that transactions generally take longer due to more cumbersome processes. Additionally, in all but the largest areas, nobody at the bank will speak English, so you'll need to be proficient speaking Spanish, or have a friend who is, to conduct much of your business. All the account forms are in Spanish, all the rules and restrictions in Spanish, so banking in Mexico can seem difficult to someone who doesn't know much of the lingo.

All banks now offer Internet banking and most also will allow you to pay utilities online, or automatically if you select that option. That can be handy if you're away for months at a time, as the power company still wants its money whether you're in-country or not.

Once you're past the account opening hurdle, things operate more or less like banks did in the U.S. thirty years ago. Banks in Mexico aren't really in the money lending business aside from the odd mortgage or credit card, they are in the taking your deposit business, or giving you cash business. Because of this, you can expect more and higher fees, as they have to earn their keep somehow.

Mexican banking is relatively new, as most natives had a deep distrust of banks due to currency devaluations and a lack of regulatory infrastructure. That's all changed over the last couple of decades, and now it's rare to encounter a native who doesn't have at least a checking account.

Credit cards are also still relatively new, and rates are nosebleed levels, as in thirty or forty percent or more interest per year. This is due to a high default rate (responsible bill paying is also somewhat new to natives) as well as a lack of any restrictions on what the CC companies can charge. The best bet if you get a Mexican credit card is to have it automatically paid from your checking, in full, each month.

Opening an account is straightforward, however be warned that if you're a U.S. citizen you'll have your passport info taken. This is significant because Mexico has information-sharing agreements with the U.S. under FACTA, so any thoughts of being able to duck the IRS are fantasies. Just assume that your activity will be on all radar screens, and check the appropriate box on your tax form every year indicating that you have a foreign account.

There any number of banks to choose from, including BBVA Bancomer, Citi Banamex, HSBC, Scotiabank, Banco Santander, Banorte, and Intercam. Most are at least part-owned by U.S. banks.

Using ATMs in Mexico can be expensive, with rates as high as two to three percent per transaction. Rates can be higher for cash advances. Best bet is to use only the ATM from your bank's branches, as accessing local accounts is generally low or no cost. If you use the ATM to access your U.S. account, you'll get a good exchange rate (close to interbank rate) but will be clipped for the transaction charge, so generally speaking it's not a good idea as you'll pay more than if you just wired a decent chunk to your Mexican account.

Speaking of wires, you can expect to pay anywhere from $20 to $30 to receive a wire, in addition to any fee charged by the sending bank, and $35 to send one.

Recently, banks have started charging a tax on cash deposits over a certain threshold – fifteen hundred dollars (or peso equivalent) as of this edition. This is due to the government attempting to crack down on the underground economy, wherein deals are done in cash in order to avoid taxes. While it's counter-intuitive that anyone in their right mind doing business in lots of cash would then go to the bank to deposit it and get charged several percent for the privilege, that's the thinking from the Mexican tax authority. My hunch is that drives the cash economy even further underground and is counter-productive, but then again, I'm not an economist or a banker, so what do I know? The point is you don't want to deposit big wads of dollars or pesos as you'll get clipped. The threshold changes fairly often, so ask at a bank for the latest numbers. Again, this only applies to cash, not wire transfers or checks or electronic transfers.

Mexican banks offer a variety of account types – checking, deposit accounts (savings accounts) that can be either "on sight" (meaning available for withdrawal anytime with no notice) or "notice" (which pay higher interest, but act like a CD in that your money is tied up for a pre-determined duration – thirty, sixty, ninety days or longer, and you generally can't withdraw the funds early), car loans, credit cards, mortgages (if you're a resident), etc.

If you're a high net worth client, most banks also offer a preferential banking service akin to private banking, where you'll have a facilitation officer fluent in English, as well as a special access window where you can bypass the line. Most banks require around a hundred-thousand-dollar average balance in your total accounts to warrant this service.

Many expats choose to use a U.S. bank like Schwab, Chase, or Fidelity because they will refund ATM fees and offer other perks on their cards, so it is worth exploring their offerings before you relocate. I have friends that have lived in Mexico for years and never bothered to open a Mexican account, preferring to use their Schwab card for charges and to pull cash. This is a painless way to bank once you get used to it, and is worth looking into.

To transfer money from a U.S. account to a Mexican account, many use services like Xoom.com, Transferwise, or Western Union. More information is available by Googling them and comparing fees and timing.

Credit and Bank Charges/Fees

Credit

Over the last decade consumer lending has become significant business in Mexico. The good news is you don't need to be a Mexican citizen to get credit in Mexico. However, you do need to be legally resident with either a temporary or permanent residence visa, and be able to prove your income. And you'll need to weigh the cost of acquiring credit with the benefits.

In addition to proving your residency, you'll also need a bank or credit reference from your home country – one is good, two better. You should get at least one letter from your U.S. or Canadian Bank before going in to open an account, as its presence in your file is virtually mandatory for most banking and all credit transactions.

Credit can be applied for directly from a bank or, if you're buying durable goods (a car, tractor, etc.), the credit application can be made through the company selling you the goods.

Whether you apply directly or via a third party, you'll need to provide references and the bank will make a credit query via the National Credit Bureau. The Credit Bureau is the sole keeper of credit info in the country, and is essential to the operation of the Mexican credit system, keeping historical info on individuals and rating them according to payment history, income, etc.

It's a good idea to have at least a year's worth of bank statements from your home bank, along with the aforementioned letter or reference from the bank before you open an account. Copies will go into your file, and it'll save you the hassle of trying to get them long distance, so bring them with you when you come down.

Sales Tax on Interest and Charges

All bank charges, fees, commissions, and credit interest are subject to sales tax in Mexico. Mexican sales tax is known as IVA: *Impuesto del Valor Agregado* (Value Added Tax). In Mexico, your real rate of interest is the CAT (for an explanation of CAT, see the following section) plus sales tax. It's currently sixteen percent in all Mexico.

Because sales tax is applied to interest, fees and bank commissions, the cost of credit—whether it's on a credit card, car loan, personal loan or other any form of non-mortgage credit—is higher than the rate quoted on literature or examples of repayment schedules.

CAT – "Costo Anual Total" or 'Real' Cost

Whenever you get any form of credit in Mexico, there are always a bevy of charges, commissions, and fees that get added to the loan amount. For years, banks were quoting interest rates and interest charges while keeping the fees, commissions and other charges hidden in the small print. To counter this, in 1996, the Bank of Mexico, in order to make it easier to understand the real cost of a loan, introduced a standard known as "CAT", which stands for *Costo Anual Total* (Total Annual Cost). The CAT must now be published on all literature related to a loan.

The CAT calculation can add from ten to fifty percent per year to a headline interest rate. Oddly, it doesn't add in the IVA tax, so you also need to tack that on to the published CAT for the true loan amount. If you're getting the picture that the cost of credit in Mexico is far, far higher than in the U.S. or Canada, you have an accurate understanding of how it works.

Exchanging Money

Retail banks, currency exchange houses and hotels are the most common places where foreign currencies are exchanged in Mexico. Most developed areas will have all the above.

Banks

Mexican banks are not particularly interested in engaging in currency exchange for anyone but bank clients. This is particularly true if you want to exchange more than a few hundred dollars of cash, or want to use traveler's checks. It's usually a better idea to use one of the money exchange houses if you're traveling and aren't a bank customer.

Many banks won't exchange currency unless you have an account with them, while others place restrictions on exchanges (like only certain hours). Additionally, you'll get to experience the patience-building exercise of the Mexican bank line, which can run a half hour, forty-five minutes, or an hour or more, depending upon whether it's payday or not. I only do dollar to peso exchanges from my dollar account to my peso account for this reason – the lines are enough to drive you nuts unless you have unlimited time. For exchanging cash, I'll use a money exchange house, which will give me a better rate than the bank on cash, and is far, far faster.

Money Exchange Houses

Called "*Casa de Cambio*" in Spanish, these outfits cater to tourists, and can be found in most tourist areas. The staff will usually speak at least some, if not fluent, English. They are the preferred choice for exchanging dollars for pesos, although they have to abide by ever changing anti-money laundering rules imposed to curb the U.S. "War on Drugs." Check with several different companies for rates, as they tend to be competitive and it pays to shop around. You can also ask about the latest rules regarding cash exchanges, which tend to change without warning, and fairly often.

Currency

The peso is the official national currency in Mexico. The value fluctuates daily, and sites abound that can keep you up to date on the current exchange rates, including Yahoo Finance. Bills are denominated in 20, 50, 100, 200, 500 and 1000 peso amounts, with the 1000 peso bills relatively rare. Coins come in .10, .5, 1, 2, 5 and 10 peso denominations, with the smallest being 10 *centavos* and 50 *centavos* (cents).

Most everywhere in Baja you can use dollars or pesos interchangeably, with the caveat being you'll get taken to the cleaners by most restaurants, gas stations, and stores on the exchange rate; you'll quickly discover their rate is at least ten to fifteen percent below the bank rate, so of course they love it if you pay in dollars – it's an automatic net boost to their profit, with no effort. It's always best to exchange money at one of the aforementioned Exchange Houses, or to do a dollar to peso account exchange at your bank.

Dollar bills are fine, but nobody will accept U.S. coins, so stick to paper money and leave the nickels and quarters in your suitcase.

On mainland Mexico, nobody will accept dollars, so you will have to carry pesos at all times.

Mexican bills come in bright colors and different sizes, so aren't easily confused in terms of denomination. The 20 peso bills are the smallest and are bright blue. 50 peso bills are pink, 100 peso bills red, 200 peso bills green, 500 peso bills brown or blue, and 1000 peso bills purple (the brand new ones are more blueish).

A note on bringing cash into Mexico. In theory, you shouldn't transport more than $10,000.00 in cash or cash equivalent per person or you will need to declare the amount. In practice, nobody is doing strip searches at the airports in Mexico upon arrival from the US or Canada, so there is virtually no way to detect money on your person – say you fly in with $40,000.00 in U.S. dollars in your cargo shorts, but forget to check the box – you'll find you just breeze through customs. Even if you get the red light when you push the customs button, the customs agent will do a cursory search of your luggage, and that's it. I'm not advising that you do this, mind you, however it is interesting to note how lax customs is on stopping you from bringing a pile of money or diamonds into the country, provided it is on your person. And if you're driving, obviously nobody is going to be doing a pat-down search, especially if going southbound. I've got acquaintances who have driven down with $500K in gold bullion in their car and had no issues.

Again, I'm not saying you should bring large quantities of cash with you, rather am merely pointing out the mechanisms for stopping you from doing so, which are essentially non-existent. My formal advice is of course to comply with all laws and rules at all times – but if you forget, there won't be anyone to report it to, is the message.

Social Security/IMSS

Americans can have their social security checks automatically deposited into their U.S. accounts, or their Mexican accounts, which makes the logistics of accessing the loot pretty straightforward in Mexico. From the Social Security website:

"You may want your Social Security payment to be directly deposited into your account at either a financial institution in the country where you live or a U.S. financial institution. Even if you use the direct deposit service, you must keep us informed of any change in your current residence address.

Direct deposit has several advantages. You never have to worry about your check being delayed in the mail, lost or stolen. With direct deposit you receive your payment much faster than if you're paid by check (usually one to three weeks faster than check deliveries). You also avoid check cashing and currency conversion fees. Some countries where direct deposit payments are available include:

- Anguilla
- Antigua & Barbuda
- Australia
- Austria
- Bahama Islands
- Barbados
- Belgium
- British Virgin Islands
- Canada
- Cayman Islands
- Cyprus
- Denmark
- Dominican Republic
- Finland
- France
- Germany
- Greece
- Grenada
- Haiti
- Hong Kong
- Hungary
- Ireland
- Israel
- Italy
- Jamaica
- Japan
- Malta
- Mexico
- Netherlands
- Netherlands Antilles
- New Zealand
- Norway
- Panama
- Poland
- Portugal
- St. Kitts & Nevis
- St. Lucia
- St. Vincent & the Grenadines
- South Africa
- Spain
- Sweden
- Switzerland
- Trinidad & Tobago
- United Kingdom

(This list of countries is subject to change from time to time. For the latest information, please visit:
socialsecurity.gov/international/countrylist6.htm
or contact your nearest U.S. Social Security office, U.S. Embassy or consulate.)

To determine if direct deposit or other forms of electronic payment are available in the country where you live—or to sign up for direct deposit—contact the nearest U.S. Embassy or consulate or U.S. Social Security office, or write to the Social Security

Administration, P.O. Box 17769, Baltimore, Maryland 21235-7769, USA."

Mexican social security is called IMSS, and is only available to Mexican citizens or those with a permanent residence status, who are fully immigrated and have paid into the system via their job. Health care under the system is free at the IMSS hospitals after paying an annual fee, however care can vary from very good to marginal, depending upon which area of Mexico you reside in – in Zapopan and Colima it is quite good. Baja, not so much. Merida is pretty good, Chapala you have to go to Guadalajara for anything serious. Waits for care can be long, as with all "free" healthcare systems, and facilities are generally crowded at any time of the day or night.

Most Gringo residents choose to get private healthcare coverage, as the private hospitals in Mexico tend to be quite good, again depending upon which town you live in. The point is one can choose to rely upon the free care if one so chooses and qualifies, or one can buy insurance for a relatively nominal amount.

Automobile Ownership

Most expats in Mexico own at least one car. There are a number of ways to do so once you live here. In Baja, you can choose to leave your car registered in your home state in the U.S. or you can change the state of registration to one that has minimal or no requirements for insurance and smog checks, you can import your vehicle, or you can buy a

Mexican vehicle. On mainland, you're limited to buying a Mexican vehicle.

The good news is that a new car in Mexico is roughly 30-50%% cheaper than it is in the U.S. due to the mountain of hidden taxes baked into every U.S. vehicle. Even luxury vehicles like a Mercedes, as an example will be far less expensive, so if you have a dream car (as long as it's not Italian or British, which cost considerably more due to tariffs on those countries' automobiles) Mexico is the place to buy it!

Baja

Technically, once you have a residence card (temp or permanent), you're obligated to only drive a Mexican-plated car. That's the letter of the law. Ninety-nine percent of all expats in Baja don't observe this rule, and instead choose to drive using their U.S. or Canadian license, keeping their native state plates.

One of the big drawbacks to this approach is most states have annual smog check requirements in order to get registration tags, meaning you'll need to drive back to that state in order to register your car. Additionally, most states also require proof of American insurance in order to register the car. This combines to create an expensive and cumbersome ownership experience, saddling you with the cost of insurance, at least one driving trip back to the states per year, and the expense of doing a smog check.

Many expat Americans choose to re-register their vehicles in states that don't have a requirement for a smog check or insurance. A favorite is South Dakota, where the cost of registration is truly nominal for most vehicles ($35 or so), and where no insurance is required provided you aren't driving on South Dakota roads...and no smog check is required either. There is a facilitator who advertises with some regularity in the Gringo Gazette offering this service, and for most his one-time fee is a bargain in saved insurance costs and hassles. His info is bobjankovics@gmail.com – I don't necessarily endorse him in any way, however he's proved reliable for thousands of Baja residents.

Importation of vehicles is problematic and generally expensive, but can be worth it if the vehicle is a truck (trucks are considered work vehicles and are subject to far lower immigration fees) that's at least five years old, but no older than ten years. The only vehicles allowed for importation have to fall into that age range. While ostensibly the older vehicles are more pollutant than the newer ones, justifying the ten-year rule, there's absolutely no reason for the "at least five years old" rule other than to protect the new car dealer monopolies in Mexico from competition from abroad. As with all protectionist tariffs, they generally exist solely to benefit a small group of special interests at the expense of the general public. That's true in all countries, and Mexico is no different.

Costs to import automobiles change almost daily, so the best way to gauge whether it makes sense to import your vehicle is to check with one of the myriad companies that handle importation. Many of the shipping companies can handle or facilitate this. One huge pain in the bottom is that often the vehicle has to sit in an impound yard in Tijuana for a week or two as it's imported, which isn't exactly convenient if you've decided to settle in Southern Baja and want to import your car at the end of your first year there. Importation in my experience works best if you're going to buy a vehicle in the States from a private party, and then drive it to TJ for the process. Otherwise it probably isn't worth the difficulty.

Buying a vehicle in Baja is simple, however one of the big issues with many cars for sale is they tend to be salvage vehicles purchased at auction in California or Arizona or Texas, and then repaired in Mexico to look like new. Even if the job is done well, it's not the same as buying a vehicle that hasn't ever been in an accident, and the unknowns are substantial – consider that you don't have any idea whether the car you're considering was underwater for four days, or the frame was bent and then straightened, permanently weakening it, or only driven on Sundays by a little old lady.

Additionally, Baja vehicles tend to see a lot of rough terrain, i.e. dirt roads, trails, massively pot-holed streets, etc. so their suspensions can be suspect. And finally, the Baja *manana* attitude applies to routine service, so oil changes and preventative maintenance can be lackadaisical at best, and downright dangerous at worst. If I was going to buy a car in Mexico (and I have) I would look for a newer car from a private party that was bought new in Mexico, even if the car commands a premium price, as the likelihood is the original owner serviced their considerable investment at the dealer, with the stamps to prove it.

Last but not least when it comes to car options, I'd avoid rental car sales at all costs. I've seen firsthand the sort of treatment they get from adventurous renters intent on exploring the most brutal terrain in Baja using a rental, and you couldn't get me to buy one if you held a gun to my head.

Registering a vehicle in Baja, once imported, is actually dirt cheap and relatively painless. As an example, I paid $20 for a six-year-old Ford F-150 annual registration with Baja plates, so there's a definite cost advantage over anything but the South Dakota option.

Make copies of your registration and all pertinent documents, including your driver's license, and keep them in a safe place in your home, so in case the car is stolen or you lose the original paperwork, you at least have somewhere to start in re-documenting.

Mainland Mexico

On mainland Mexico, you don't have the latitude you do in Baja, and you're limited to buying a "national" car that was originally sold new in Mexico. While there used to be ways to import a car on mainland if you were willing to pay the right person to look the other way, those days are gone, and there's only one way to go as of this writing, which is buy a new or used Mexican vehicle.

Whichever you choose, you'll receive the original "factura" when you pay, which is the title to the vehicle, for all intents and purposes. Whomever holds that document legally owns the car, so I would keep it in an extremely safe place. If you lose it, you're looking at months of grief to bet a new one. If you're buying a used car, you have to basically establish the chain of custody of the vehicle, which includes obtaining all registration proofs for every year it's been in existence, the

ID of the prior owners, and a "tarjeta de circulacion," which is the circulation card you would use to prove the registration is current and that you own the car if stopped by a cop. You'll also require insurance documentation, which you should keep in the vehicle. Liability insurance will be required, at a minimum, for any car you buy.

If you want a more detailed description of the documents required to buy a used car in Mexico, I would try the following site, which has a credible checklist of items you'll be well advised to follow in the purchase process: https://mexlaw.ca/foreigners-registering-vehicle-mexico/

Automobile Insurance

U.S. car insurance isn't valid in Mexico, so you're required by law to have Mexican insurance. In the event of an accident, if you don't have Mexican insurance you'll go straight to jail, and a Mexican jail is actually worse than anything you can imagine. So don't risk it – it's a very bad bet to drive without insurance here.

Fortunately, car insurance is about half the cost as in the U.S., so this is another instance where you'll save a bundle by moving to Mexico. There are numerous providers on the Internet – just do a search for Mexican Auto Insurance, and you'll get hundreds of hits.

You'll want full coverage, and also want to limit your coverage to Baja if that's where you're going to stay, as otherwise the cost skyrockets if you include mainland Mexico. Only liability insurance is required to drive legally, but I would advise the full monte, as if you're involved in a serious accident you could face considerable issues with only liability. So while you can get away with the minimum, I wouldn't unless you're high net worth and could pay cash to get yourself out of any bind you find yourself in.

Insurance is available in daily, monthly, quarterly and annual increments, so if you decide to drive down to Mexico to explore, you don't have to commit to a year's worth. Additionally, if you're not the type to plan ahead, there are dozens of shops near the Mexican border advertising auto insurance, so you can get it as you're about to cross over. And speaking of crossing over, again, you'll need a passport to get in and out, thus a driver's license won't be enough. Make a copy of your passport, too, just in case, and ensure it doesn't expire before you plan to return to the U.S. or you'll have problems.

General Automobile Tips

It's a good idea to get some sort of SUV if you're going to live in Baja, as many of the roads leave much to be desired, and quite a few of the more interesting areas completely lack pavement. While four-wheel drive is a great option, it's not absolutely necessary as long as you're careful about where you're driving. As an example, I've only really had to use my four-wheel capability once in the last five years, and that was in Loreto when I drove out a little too far on a road leading to the beach, and found myself in sand. Other than that one time, I've enjoyed a lot of off-road driving, but I've never *needed* the four wheel capability.

On mainland, an SUV also isn't a bad idea, although depending on the roads, isn't necessary. Look around wherever you're going to settle and use your head before buying.

For Baja, any car you bring down should be equipped with off-road tires if possible, with the knobbiest tread available. All-terrain tires are good, mud-terrain tires are better. Especially in Southern Baja, there's sand and dirt on many of the road surfaces, as well as many deep and treacherous potholes, and inevitable chunks of steel, nails, screws, bits of rebar, parts of cars that fell off, etc. When it rains, you'll thank me for this advice, as it's not unusual to encounter a foot or two of water within ten minutes of hard rain starting, and normal street tires are all but useless in the ensuing mud and muck. Sporty rims with low profile tires are great for streets in the U.S., but the first time you hit a pothole doing fifty and blow out the sidewall you'll appreciate why you don't see many in Baja.

On mainland, road conditions will vary greatly. Chapala and Colima aren't great as they use volcanic rock for pavement in many areas. Zapopan is good. Merida is generally good. Toll roads you would take between cities are largely very good – as well maintained as the best highways in the U.S., and in many cases, better. I never take the free roads where toll roads are available, as the toll roads are safe and well patrolled, whereas the free roads are anything goes, and I never feel all that interested in trying my luck. Whenever you hear a horror story about robberies or worse, it's on a free road. My advice is give them a pass and pay the toll every time, as you'll save not only on risk to life and limb, but also to your car's suspension when you find yourself hitting foot deep potholes that appear out of nowhere on the free roads.

Gasoline is plentiful, and offered in two grades by Pemex, the national oil company: Green/unleaded (*Verde*) or Red/premium (*Roja*). Both are available in all but a few remote areas. Most people run the green, as modern cars will automatically adjust the fuel to air mixture to compensate for lower octane even if the manuals recommend premium gas, however check online or with a mechanic to be sure about your specific car. I've found the red/premium is actually better made/cleaner, at least that's what my mechanic tells me, however other than anecdotal evidence I can't make that claim with complete certainty. I know people who've had problems with their injectors and had the gas quality blamed by their service guy, however I've never experienced any problems driving here for many years, so it's anyone's guess as to what's accurate. Other branded stations are now popping up in some states, but I've found that pricing is still relatively monolithic regardless of which purveyor I choose, so I opt to fill up where convenient whenever I hit a quarter tank.

Diesel is available at some stations, however there are never any guarantees. I personally wouldn't own a diesel vehicle in Mexico, as even though they are more reliable engines, there are few competent mechanics with germane experience on them, thus if something goes wrong, it's likely to stay wrong for a long time. Add to this that parts availability in-country is likely to be nil for diesel engines, and you can see why I avoid them.

Since deregulation, other companies have stations in Mexico

as well, and can include Mobil, Oxxo, and a host of other private operators. Prices can vary significantly by region, but are generally within a tight band in any metro area.

All stations are full service – there's no such thing as self-service pumping in Mexico, except for a handful of very remote stations. It's customary to tip the attendant a few pesos for filling up and washing your windshield (*limpiar el cristal*) – I usually tip 5 to 10 pesos on a 1000 peso fill-up, as the attendant is making minimum wage, which is about $5 a day, and really earns their living off the tips.

Gas stations are regulated and checked annually by Profeco, the consumer protection agency, however it's not unknown for the accuracy of the pumps to vary considerably from station to station. One recent survey in the Cabo area had a 5 gallon can filled with anywhere from 5 gallons to 6.4 gallons, despite the physical impossibility of the latter. So be alert when you fill up, and if you seem to have gotten way more fuel than you normally use, note to yourself never to use that station again. You can complain to Profeco and maybe they'll investigate at some point, however there's no guaranteed recourse other than voting with your wallet, so again, caveat emptor.

Another unfortunate truism in the tourist areas is the gas station attendants are magicians at pulling currency cheating. You'll give them 500 pesos for your 300 peso fill-up, and they'll distract you or do some sleight of hand, and give you 100 fewer pesos for change, claiming you only gave them 400 pesos, or worse yet demand another 250 pesos, claiming you gave them a 50 peso note, not a 500. This happens with alarming regularity to obvious Gringo visitors (a rental car is a giveaway, as is a car with foreign plates packed full of belongings), and again, there's no real recourse. You can yell, argue with the attendant, threaten to call the police, but in the end it's your word (the Gringo) against the local's (the native, who is probably a friend of the neighborhood cop), so you're wasting your breath.

Best is to always get out of your vehicle and specify a peso amount, watch them zero the pump and enter that amount in the pre-programmed keypad, then watch the gas go in. When you hand over your money, state the amount you want back in change before letting go of the cash – that way there's an understanding of how much the attendant owes you, which he has to acknowledge before taking the money, and which he can challenge as wrong while you both have your hands on it (assuming there's going to be a challenge). At this point any fun and games will be over, as he'll know you understand the scams, and he won't try anything, preferring unsuspecting prey.

Preventative maintenance is critical with any vehicle, as the road conditions can be harsh, and you want your car in top condition. Regular oil changes are a must, as are air filter changes, or at the very least, blowing out the air filter every month with compressed air. Dust is far more prevalent in Mexico than the U.S., and after a month in even the cleanest towns your air filter will be filthy and choked with dust, reducing fuel efficiency and causing a host of long-term issues.

Before heading south of the border, you should also have your transmission serviced, including the filter changed or flushed. Driving the sometimes mountainous terrain in a fully loaded vehicle in hundred degree heat can cause a seemingly fine transmission to fail at the absolutely worst time. Once, I had a four-year-old Japanese SUV fail in the mountains due to a clogged tranny filter, even though it ran fine in the states and halfway down Baja. Apparently the strain of carting a full load up some radical hills in extreme heat caused the particulate matter in the transmission fluid to coagulate in the filter, ultimately clogging it completely, resulting in a total transmission failure. That's a lot of fun on the side of a mountain in August in hundred- and four-degree heat, with pets and a child in the car, in an area where cell service doesn't work due to the mountains, and with maybe one car every couple hours passing by. Trust me when I tell you that you don't want to ever be in that situation.

Carrying a spare tire is a no brainer. Something not as obvious, however, is that tires degrade from the constant sun at an accelerated rate, so even if you have a ton of tread left, they'll be suspect in roughly half the time they would last in the States. You should make a habit out of inspecting your tires every four months to see how they're holding up, as well as checking the pressure. Blowouts are never fun.

You should also carry a basic maintenance kit with tools, aerosol tire inflation goop, an oil filter, some brake fluid, a spare quart of oil, and a spare quart of tranny fluid. If you have wheel locks, locate the key and make sure you remember where you put it. Confirm you have a jack, and that it works. If you don't have a full sized spare tire, buy a rim that will fit the car and put a real tire on it – you may wind up having to drive eighty miles in harsh conditions on that spare, so one of those doughnuts intended for twenty miles of smooth surface streets isn't going to serve you well.

Investing in "The Club" steering wheel security device is a good idea, as is never keeping anything of value in your car. If a kid breaks the window in the middle of the night trying to find something easy to steal, you're better off if he goes away empty handed. Obviously, sporting a thousand-dollar stereo system would be a poor idea for the same reason.

Finding competent mechanics can be problematic, as while all of them will claim to be adept, in my experience a significant number shouldn't be allowed to hold a wrench. I wish I could offer better advice than, "Ask around", but that is really how you need to go about it. One of the problems, as I've said before, is that it's culturally frowned upon to disappoint another, thus mechanics will claim to be able to diagnose or have fixed something when they have no such expertise. Of course, there's also the problem that some will invent problems in order to pad their wallet, however the larger issue is usually the mechanic just doesn't no how to say, "No."

Dealerships are usually pretty safe and sure bets, as their mechanics have undergone specialized training and certification, however even dealerships can have the same issue – they don't want to admit they don't know or couldn't figure it out, partly out of machismo, and partly in order to avoid disappointing you. If you put out feelers among the expats in your area, you'll invariably hear the same name come up over and over, and that's generally your best bet for a private mechanic. Of course, at the end of the day, there's always the grim and expensive alternative of shipping the vehicle by carrier back up to the border and to an American mechanic, however hopefully you won't have to do so.

The other issue you'll have with private mechanics is that while Mexicans are extremely resourceful at making things work with a dearth of the correct parts, it's not always a recipe for a successful long-term fix to have things "jury rigged." I've had to have four different muffler shops work on one of my trucks to correct an exhaust leak – each one reporting a successful outcome, but then the problem returned in a short period. The issue was that unbeknownst to me, three of the four used incorrect seals or bolts or gaskets, which only temporarily corrected the leak. In the U.S. you could feel comfortable taking the vehicle back to the same shop and complaining, however here what that amounts to is taking the car back to the same guy who couldn't figure out how to do it right the last time, hoping he develops some new breakthrough expertise he clearly lacked earlier. Not a good bet. And forget about getting your money back – it was spent that evening, trust me on that.

That's the overview on everything you need to know about vehicles and Mexico. In a later chapter we'll discuss driving idiosyncrasies, and I'll tell you some horror stories to illustrate why you have to expect the unexpected at all times on Mexican roads.

Chapter 6

–

Health Care, Insurance, Medication, Elective Care, Dying in Mexico

Health Care Overview

Gringos will find that the cost of Mexican health care providers is significantly lower than their U.S. counterparts. What follows is an overview of the current status of hospitals, doctors and dentists, and the pros and cons of each category of practitioner.

Some areas of Mexico have special concerns, like scorpion bites, snakebites, or mosquito-borne Dengue fever or Malaria or Zika. Consult the online message boards and health bulletins for specifics on your target area.

Hospitals

Mexico has two types of hospitals – IMSS (social security/public), and private.

This section will focus on private hospitals, as IMSS is the public system, and the quality of the care can vary tremendously depending on the area and the doctor. Most Mexicans with any kind of money opt for private facilities, which is my advice to anyone reading. If cost is your number one concern, and you're willing to take whatever is on offer, and subject yourself to long waits and iffy care, IMSS might be in your wheelhouse. That is not to say there aren't fine doctors in the system, but as with any bell curve, the best will typically be where the money is, and the mediocre will go wherever they can get a job, which is often the public system. Use your head on this one. With costs as low as they are at quality private facilities, this isn't where I'd want to try to save a few bucks, especially if I had anything seriously wrong.

Hospitals in Mexico can vary significantly in terms of the age of their equipment, cleanliness, and overall competence. Much like the rest of the world in that regard. Obviously, the more affluent areas have the more developed private hospitals, as the clientele has more money and demands a higher standard of care. Most hospitals are suitable for minor surgery (burst appendix, car accident fallout, trips and falls), however most Gringos prefer to travel to the U.S. for serious care. Locals will often opt to get treated at hospitals in Mexico City or Guadalajara for serious situations, such as heart surgery, neurosurgery, cancer, etc.

The standard of care in Mexico improves every year, and many of the doctors are first rate, however there are limitations in the available technologies as well as acumen – the heavy hitters generally work in the largest metro areas, where the market will bear higher prices and more cases. As I mentioned earlier, public hospitals are generally at the bottom of the totem pole in terms of quality of care (which is reflected in their low annual cost), while the better private hospitals will have equipment and standards comparable to top flight facilities in the U.S. or Canada.

Treatment costs are lower than the U.S., however how much lower typically varies depending upon where the facility is located. The farther from a major tourist venue, the less expensive. Payment in private hospitals is cash or credit card, with some private insurance accepted, depending upon the issuer. Usually for tourists a private hospital will demand cash or CC payment, and then you get reimbursed by your insurance company. This is to save them the considerable difficulty and cost involved with dealing with foreign insurance companies whose motivation is to stall paying anything as long as possible. Permanent residents can get Mexican insurance that will cover their hospital stay with little or no money out of pocket at fractions of the price of U.S. policies.

Normally, the cost to go to the hospital in Mexico are far lower than in the U.S., and service is far better.

As an example of typical costs for a hospital visit in Mexico, a visit to the emergency room at any of the larger private hospitals in Guadalajara might cost $35 to $40, not counting any ancillary tests. In Baja it might be more like $40-$50, in Colima or Merida more like $30-$35. You'll often be seen within five minutes or so if you aren't bleeding out, and in ten seconds if you are. Contrast that to the cost and time you'll experience in any U.S. hospital, and it gets very obvious very quickly how badly broken the U.S. health system is.

A bed in a private hospital in Guadalajara will run $100-$150 a night for a private room at a major facility, $75-$100 at a lesser one, and an ICU room will run about $250. The cost of meds and supplies are a quarter or less the cost in a US hospital, even in ICU. A year ago a friend of mine's infant had a severe respiratory infection, and had to spend five days in ICU (more expensive than adult ICU), with round-the-clock specialist care, and another five days in a private room, and the total came to $4200, including all the nebulizers, antibiotics, tests, specialist consults, etc. Or take a caesarian delivery, which at a private hospital might run $2000 all in, from admission to discharge, including the staff, anesthesiologist, gyno, two-day hospital stay, etc.

A broken hand will cost $125 or so, including X-rays and cast, in an ER. A minor surgery like a gash from a surfboard might run the same. A buddy of mine who is an avid surfer from California got slashed by a board while in Cabo, which is more expensive than most of Mexico. Eight stitches later, his bill was $140. The same thing happened to him a few years later in Laguna Beach, and the bill was $4200 for the same procedure. I couldn't make this up.

Here is a partial list of surgery costs at a top-quality hospital in Guadalajara, as a comparison tool for you to use. All prices are in U.S. dollars, at an exchange rate of approximately 22 pesos to the dollar:

Appendectomy is $2200.
Tummy Tuck is $1800.
Blepharoplasty is $950.
Colonoscopy is $750.
Craniotomy is $2800.
Hernioplasty is $1700.
Hysterectomy from $1800-$2200.
Mastectomy $1900. Bi-lateral is $2500.
Prostatectomy $2400.

Rhinoplasty $1250.
Thyroidectomy $2000.

A heart bypass will cost $3000. In the U.S. it will average $123,000, plus a host of up-charges. As I said before, a private room in Mexico will run $150, whereas in the U.S., $3500. It is small wonder that 60% of all bankruptcies in the U.S. are medically related.

Doctors

A trip to the doctor, if he's a specialist, will cost around $35 or so. Maybe $40 in more expensive towns. If it's a general practitioner for something like a sore throat, it can be as low as $10 – many pharmacies have a doctor right next door, who sees locals for $5 or $10 a visit, or in some cases, purely for a tip. I tend to take the high road for my occasional healthcare woes, preferring to splurge on the $40 guy with twenty years of experience if I'm really sick. Almost all the physicians in Baja speak perfect English. This isn't necessarily so on mainland (except in Zapopan, where most are bi-lingual), however if tourism is part of the environment, it's likely English is spoken. Ask around the expat community in your town for English speaking doctors if there's any doubt in your mind.

A complete annual physical, including all blood tests and X-rays, at the place I frequent, runs me a whopping $160. When I was in the U.S., same tests came in at five times the cost. I understand I could get the same tests done for as low as $130 if I really wanted to shop everything around, but at the end of the day I'll pay the extra for the best folks in the region performing the work.

Trip to the Dermatologist? $40, including freezing or lasering off that suspicious growth, in Zapopan.

Ear, nose and throat exam? $35 in Zapopan.

Cardiologist? $45. Treadmill and Halter? $60 in Zapopan.

EKG in a hospital or a specialist? $35-$40.

You can quickly see how costs in Mexico are a fifth to a twentieth of the cost of equivalent care in the U.S. That's why I don't tend to sweat a trip to the doctor anymore. For the price of a few supersize meals at a fast food restaurant, I can take care of staying healthy, so it's a bargain. I believe most of the cost differential can be boiled down to two factors: The plaintiffs bar in the U.S., and medicine as a business there.

Most of the U.S. doctors I know in private practice pay unbelievable malpractice insurance premiums, as every other case has an attorney waiting in the wings to sue at the drop of a hat. I'm talking premiums in the many hundreds of thousands, or even millions of dollars annually. That price gets passed on to the patient, which is why a trip to the doctor in California might wind up costing you $150, for what can be had in Mexico for $30. Ironically, doctors in Mexico spend far more time with patients than their U.S. counterparts, primarily because time in the U.S. is, well, money, whereas not so much in Mexico.

Which brings me to the machine that is American medicine –

a money machine. If you're a doctor, and you can limit your patient time to five minutes instead of fifteen, you can see far more patients per hour. That will help pay for the expensive nurses and front office staff – jobs that pay ¼ or less as much in Mexico. So instead of dispensing health care, many physicians are forced into creating a treadmill where patients get cursory exams, and then it's on to the next one. I've discovered that the great fallacy of U.S. medicine, which is touted as some of the best in the world, is that actual patient care is performed by the lowest personnel on the food chain, thus all that great care is delivered by a truculent nurse or nurse's assistant who would rather be texting her boyfriend than dealing with you. In Mexico it's a bit different, in that doctors are older fashioned, and spend considerable time with their patients, as much as three to five times as much time, getting to understand their needs, fears, and ailments.

On the flip side, I've also found that patient history recording is generally sub-par in Mexico. Doctors and hospitals rarely ask for a complete list of medications you're taking, and sometimes skip even obvious steps like asking what you're allergic to. It's best to be pro-active (also true in the U.S.) and present the doctor with a list of all meds taken, and any allergies. That forces them to consider those items, which can fall through the cracks.

On balance, having lived all over the world, I'd put Mexican medical care at a 7.5 overall, with the U.S. at a hard 8. The difference is generally in the availability of the very latest technology, where the U.S. has an advantage.

Dentists

I have to say that my dentists in Mexico are among the best I've ever seen. Let me preface that with the observation that I hate going to the dentist, dislike needles intensely, will do about anything to avoid pain, and generally procrastinate on anything dentally-oriented. When I'm going blind from pain, it's time to see the dentist. Up until then, I'll wish it away, go into denial, try to convince myself I can wait it out and it will miraculously get better, etc.

My dentist in Cabo San Lucas is light years ahead of any dentist I ever saw in the U.S. And I'm talking seriously pricey guys in the most expensive areas of Southern California.

I go into the office, where the staff speaks good English, and he has a digital X-ray system, cleans my teeth with ultrasound instead of hand tools, uses a computer-guided anesthetic delivery system where the needle goes into the gum automatically with little bursts of anesthetic delivered in advance of the puncturing so you never feel any needle or pain, has a laser to remove cavities and fillings (as opposed to a drill), and can make a crown in the office in about an hour instead of sending out to a lab and waiting a week while you wear a temporary.

His rates are about fifty percent below an American dentist. The reason he isn't seventy percent below is because he's the most modern in town.

Others are more like sixty to eighty percent below the cost of American dentists. Again, because I'm a coward, I'll pay more to feel less. It's worth it to me.

Bargain hunters routinely cross the border from San Diego to TJ to have their dental care performed, braving the cartel violence and general destitution of much of that area to save the sixty percent. Especially when it comes to recurring costs like braces, the difference can be thousands and thousands of dollars.

By way of example, a set of braces in Cabo, again, the most expensive area of Baja, might run $2300 or slightly higher, depending upon the circumstance. On mainland, same thing would be in the $1500-$1900 range. Contrast that to the U.S. The difference is pronounced.

So the good news is that dental care is relatively inexpensive, and of generally high quality in the more populated areas.

Opticians

Throw a rock in any decent sized town, and you're likely to hit an optician.

There are any number of chains operating here, as well as opticians in Sam's Club, Costco and City Club, and myriad independent opticians plying their trade.

Costs run about seventy percent of what they run in the U.S., and you can get anything from eye exams and glasses or contact lenses, to advanced laser surgery for vision correction.

Shop around, as prices vary. One note is that some of the big box store opticians will approximate your prescription rather than getting it perfect, if it's an oddball (mine is), which is annoying as the lenses won't ever be quite right. This is one of those areas where you have to double-check what was delivered against what was ordered, because I've had instances where my lenses were different enough when placed on the scope (Costco, you suck) as to be useless to me. It's usually the fault of the lab, which uses standard lenses versus custom, and not the prescription. Again, nobody wants to tell you that they can't deliver what you asked for, so you are your last line of defense in keeping your vendors honest.

Health Insurance

Private health insurance is readily available in Mexico, from a host of providers, at a considerably lower premium cost than comparable insurance in the U.S.

As in the U.S., premiums are paid monthly, and are higher based on the deductible chosen, as well as age and risk factors like smoking. You get a discount if you pay annually.

Among the many companies providing health insurance in Mexico are ING Mexico, New York Life Seguros Monterrey, Royal & Sun Alliance, MetLife and DVK

This is by no means an exhaustive list.

There are also insurance policies that include flight service via air ambulance to either mainland or the U.S. in the case of a dire emergency. There are numerous brokers online who offer the full gamut of choices. For older folks, the peace of mind of knowing they can be flown to the U.S. or to a major medical center on mainland Mexico may well be worth the premium. I personally have this sort of policy, even though I understand that the odds favor I will never need to use it. Again, peace of mind commands a price, and I'm fine with that. Check the Web for brokers who can offer a smorgasbord of healthcare options, not just for Mexico, but also for all Latin America, if you're planning to travel a lot.

The bad news is your Medicare and Medicaid are not accepted in Mexico. The good news is that due to the cost differential, it largely shouldn't matter much.

Many expats elect to pay into the national health care scheme, called IMSS, which requires that you be a resident (either temporary or permanent). You pay a low fee once a year, and all care from that point on is free. The problem is that quality of care can vary depending on locale, from quite good to abysmal. Because it is a public health system, the quality isn't subject to market forces, where customers can vote with their feet and select superior providers. You have no choice in your doctor, and must take whomever you are assigned, whether he graduated at the top of his class, or the bottom. I personally wouldn't ever use IMSS, but many do because of the price. If cost is a real constraint for you, it might be worth investigating as it will be considerably less expensive than private hospitals, and will generally include free medication at the IMSS pharmacy for widely available drugs with a prescription. You can get more information by going to the IMSS website: **http://www.imss.gob.mx/**

Medication

Most medications requiring a prescription in the U.S. and Canada are available over the counter in Mexico, at far lower prices. Generic drugs are especially inexpensive. Prices can be as much as ninety percent lower. The good news is that most medications will cost far less on a pure price basis than in the U.S. The not so good news is that many company-sponsored health care plans in the U.S. cover much of the cost of many drugs, so the co-pay may be lower than the pure cost to buy the drug in Mexico, although not always – I've sourced drugs for visiting friends which were a quarter or a fifth of the cost of their U.S. co-pay, which just highlights what a racket healthcare there is. Also, Mexico tends to be a few years behind the U.S. on boutique or novel drugs, so the very latest cutting-edge treatments may not be available in as timely a manner as north of the border.

For the vast majority of patients, the net cost is still far lower. In rare instances, where many relatively new drugs are involved, the cost may be at parity, or some of the drugs may just not be available. I'm talking esoteric medications, not mainstream.

As I said, most meds don't require a prescription. The exceptions are antibiotics, which recently became a class of drugs requiring a prescription (to prevent drug resistant strains of bacteria from developing), and CNS depressants or opioids, like Vicodin or Valium or Xanax or Ambien. Given the cost of a doctor's visit, though, even those are readily available.

One thing I've noticed is that you have to pay attention to

expiration dates, as sometimes Mexico is at the tail end of the efficacy curve. It also would serve you well to be sensitive to heat damage. Many meds shouldn't be stored above seventy or eighty degrees max, and it always kills me to walk into a pharmacy where even with the fans blowing it's a good ninety degrees plus. With companies like WalMart, City Club, Costco, and some of the large national pharmacy chains, this isn't as much of an issue, but the corner Farmacia should be treated with considerable skepticism during the summer months.

Elective Care

Increasingly, elective surgeries are becoming big business in Mexico, with private clinics offering options ranging from botox shots to facelifts, tummy tucks, liposuction, skin peels, hair removal and restoration, and every other imaginable procedure.

As expected, costs are fifty percent or less the cost of identical procedures in the U.S. Practitioners are generally highly skilled, although it's best to seek out referrals from reputable medical centers and word of mouth. Although the landscape has changed in the last decade, there are still plenty of marginal surgeons cutting away, and you don't want to be someone's bad day at the office.

For anything complicated, you're generally better advised to head to either Guadalajara, Monterrey, or Mexico City, where skill levels are likely to be higher than smaller towns. Again, ask around. My dermatologist flies to Guadalajara for anything serious, which should speak for itself.

Special Needs/Handicap Accessibility

Mexico in general doesn't have significant infrastructure for handling the handicapped. That said, the more developed areas, like Zapopan and parts of Merida and Colima, do have wheelchair accessible curbs and related improvements. It would be misleading, however, to paint a picture of a country were hundreds of millions of dollars have been spent on this. It hasn't, as in most areas just having clean water or electricity takes priority over special needs. If this is a real concern, I would advise you to look to Zapopan or Merida or Colima, and skip the more rural areas I've described, as they are going to be hit or miss, with no standard outfitting for any metro area.

Dying in Mexico

While nobody enjoys dwelling on death (although several of my exes have told me they wish for mine), it is a fact of life, and it's entirely possible, if not probable, that if you live here, you may wind up eventually dying here. Rather than belabor a list of issues those surviving you will need to contend with, I'll instead refer you to a web link that lists them, and state clearly that you want an up to date will that's notarized, as well as beneficiaries on all your bank accounts and Fideicomisos.

The URL to get more info is: expatsinmexico.com/what-to-do-when-an-expat-dies-in-mexico

Chapter 7

-

Crime & Safety, Schools, Childcare, Driving, Getting Around

Crime & Safety

We'll kick off this section by addressing the number one concern of Gringos considering Mexico as a long-term living option: Crime and safety.

It's funny for me when I read the U.S. media's portrayal of crime in Mexico. Aside from travel warnings from the Government, virtually all the coverage is sensational, and negative. This portrays a completely inaccurate picture of Mexico. It creates an impression that a trip here is akin to taking one's life in one's hands, and braving murder, kidnapping, violent assault, etc. etc. etc. I believe this is partially due to an agenda by the U.S. to make the most logical and easy choice for citizens who've decided to get the hell out, as scary and forbidding as possible, and also because negative and sensational stories sell better – let's face it, "Man Bites Dog" will get more attention than, "Weather perfect again, crime lower than most ultra-safe areas of the U.S."

The first thing you need to understand is that everything you hear about crime, violence, and Mexico, is overblown and distorted. Why do I say that? Because of the realities of distance, and the differences in communities. Just as it would be silly to you, if you lived in Orange County, California, to have friends calling worried about the killing sprees they had been reading about in Inglewood or Compton, it would be silly for you if you lived in Colima to have concerned acquaintances expressing their fears for you over the drug murders in Manzanillo. Those kidnapping and murder binges are very real and terrifying, as are murder binges in the U.S., however if you're fifty or nine-hundred or even ten miles away from their epicenter, they don't have a lot of meaning for you.

The latest stats on US citizens killed in Mexico I could find were for 2017-2018 from Stratfor, where a grand total of 238 lost their lives. Of those, 76 were homicides, and the rest were car accidents, suicides, and general accidents. Of the 76 killed, it's unknown how many were US passport carrying miscreants involved in narco-trafficking in border cities – although I suspect that accounts for a fair number, and Stratfor states as much: *"...many of the Americans murdered in places like Tijuana and Juarez were dual citizens or residents of Mexico who were involved in criminal activity..."*

To put that 76 into perspective, roughly 35 million US citizens visited Mexico during that same period. And over a million US citizens call Mexico their home. Contrast that to a place like Chicago, where 2.8 million call home, and which saw nearly 600 homicides in the same period, and you can safely say that Mexico is vastly safer than the U.S. for U.S. citizens. With about 36 million possible US citizens to murder in that period in Mexico (roughly 12% of the U.S. total population), and 76 murders, if one multiplied by 10 to roughly approximate the U.S. population, we'd see 760 murders for 350 million citizens. Contrast that to the nearly

20,000 who lost their lives in the U.S., and it would be fair to say that Mexico is 20 plus times safer than the U.S., on a broad strokes basis.

The generality portrayed in the U.S. media is, "Mexico is dangerous." Someone reading the crime reports over a typical weekend for Vegas or LA or Chicago could correctly say the same thing about those areas. Fact is, parts of Mexico are very, very dangerous. High population density, high poverty, and massive drug trafficking make that so, just as they do in the U.S. – only with the added complication of the cartels, which are bloodthirsty and ruthless, just as are organized crime syndicates everywhere.

Obviously, the trick is to avoid the areas that are dangerous. Seems like common sense to me – stay away from the guys with the guns, and you're unlikely to get shot or kidnapped.

So…my first unsurprising advice is to stay away from the guys with the guns. In Mexico, they're in the border towns and to a lesser extent along the trafficking routes up the Pacific and Atlantic coasts, because that's where the money is from trafficking dope. But mainly at the border, which is the frontier, where products with ten thousand percent margin are fought over by people who make $100 a month. You could see how it could get ugly, and my oft-repeated advice is stay well away from anything within fifty miles of the border.

Before I get a ton of angry correspondence from folks with agendas to push favoring those areas, I understand that not all places within fifty miles of the border are bad or dangerous – but I *am* sure that all places more than fifty miles away aren't nearly as bad (with the notable exception of Sinaloa, Tamaulipas, and Chihuahua, which are just downright scary bad). Thus, without trying to stay tuned to every nuance of the incredible bloodshed around the border, I'm making a very generalized statement for those looking at Mexico for the first time. Anybody who wants to try their luck exploring the border region, knock yourself out. I just won't be joining you any time soon.

The reality is once you're fifty miles south and away from the primary trafficking corridors, crime generally falls into the more benign type – car break-ins, petty theft, the occasional pick-pocket, opportunistic home break-ins, a robbery at 3AM of drunks coming back from the clubs. These types of occurrences are usually driven by poverty and youth – teens looking for some easy money with which to buy drugs or alcohol.

As I've said, the exception is the trafficking routes from north to south along the coasts, and especially the port towns, because that's where the drugs tend to arrive. As an example, Manzanillo, where the film 10 with Bo Derek was shot, is extremely dangerous as multiple cartels battle for control of the port, as it is the primary arrival point of all the ingredients for meth from China, as well as for heroin processing chemicals. It's a hub and distribution center, and so is likely to always be dangerous. But go a few miles up the coast, to Barra de Navidad, and there's virtually no crime at all, because there's no trafficking corridor running through it. Likewise, resort towns like Acapulco are best avoided, because they're the primary retail sales point for drugs to Mexicans who've driven a few hours from Mexico City to lie on the beach – and the local street dealers vying for their business are both competitive and brutal.

Make no mistake, drug trafficking hotspots are dangerous. Tijuana is a war zone some of the time. Ciudad Juarez is actively dangerous. The states immediately adjacent to the border have high levels of crime and murder due to being centers for narcotic and human trafficking.

But that's hardly all of Mexico, and it's especially not the places I've described in this book. Those locations are safe or safer than anywhere I've lived in the U.S. – Newport Beach, San Diego, Tucson, Manhattan.

Basic rules of common sense apply here. Don't be a target. Avoid flashing around lots of cash, or wearing flashy jewelry (except in Zapopan, where you're probably the poorest person you'll see). Ensure your car has an alarm, and use a steering wheel locking device like "The Club." If you like, get a dog larger than a chipmunk, as opportunistic thieves hate dogs and will go looking for easier prey. If living in a neighborhood with theft problems, ensure you have bars on the windows and good door locks. Avoid the bad areas of town, and don't go out trying to buy drugs. Don't use deserted ATMs at night, especially if there are unsavory types loitering around. Don't wander back from the club drunk on a dark street. Basic precautions you would take anywhere.

All of these apply whether we are talking about living in Houston or Chapala. Actually, Houston has a higher crime rate than any of the candidate areas I've mentioned, so the irony is that you're much more likely to be assaulted or robbed there than, say, in San Jose Del Cabo or Zapopan or

Colima or, well, anywhere away from the border danger zone. As in orders of magnitude more likely.

Now don't get me wrong. All of Mexico isn't a paradise on earth where brothers and sisters of all races and creeds dance in the streets in peace and harmony. There are areas of mainland Mexico that are fraught with danger of violent crime, largely due to the drug trade, as well as organized criminal gangs focused on kidnapping as a living. Parts of Sinaloa, Durango, Mexico City, Guerrero, and as I said earlier, along the Pacific Coast where drugs are ferried north from Central America, as well as the towns along the border are dangerous, and should be avoided. Just as parts of Detroit, and Washington D.C., and Los Angeles, and San Francisco, and Chicago, and Baltimore are very dangerous and best avoided.

But Cabo, Zapopan, Chapala, Colima, and Merida aren't those areas. I've walked down many a street in Zapopan or Cabo or Colima at four in the morning over the years, without feeling in any danger. I wouldn't even think of doing that in San Diego. Having said that, there are sections in all towns you wouldn't want to go into at night, or even during the day in some cases. The tip-off is usually when you have shanties and structures made out of packing crates instead of houses, or everything is covered with graffiti and there are bars over the bars on the windows. As with all things, use your head.

Kidnapping in southern Baja, and in Zapopan, Chapala, Merida, and Colima is virtually non-existent. It's a big problem in Mexico City and some of the other large cities, but not in the places I frequent. For the reasons why, I'll use three examples. In Baja, you're basically on an island, so there's no place to go if you kidnap someone, and because the population is small, if you're kidnapping guy, everyone likely knows it, so your game is blown. That's why they don't happen there. In Zapopan, you'd be contending with more police and security per square meter than anywhere else on earth – all of whom are there to ensure nothing bad happens. Due to the concentration of wealth, the security forces are deadly serious about protecting the residents, so to try a mugging, much less a kidnapping, would be suicide. Literally. And in Colima, there's only one highway and one secondary road running from the beaches, through the city, and north to Guadalajara. With a population of 200K, again, everyone knows who the bad guys are, and if you kidnapped anyone, they'd just seal the roads in and out and you'd have nowhere to go. So kidnapping is only viable in large, densely populated cities like Mexico City, with something like 26 million. It isn't in privileged enclaves or small towns.

In the areas of Mexico I have recommended, the murders are almost 100% narco-trafficking related. My take-away from that is don't come to Mexico trying to establish a drug trafficking conduit, and you won't be the one to disappear in the desert, never to be found. Seems simple to me, but then again, most things in Mexico do. In Zapopan there are no murders in the good areas, other than an enraged wife killing her husband for cheating. Ditto for the Lake Chapala area, and Merida, and especially Colima. In Colima, there have been a couple of high-profile killings of politicians or judges who are, by virtue of their vocations, in the line of fire of the cartels. But again, that falls under the heading of don't engage in something involving the cartels, and you won't be a target.

As covered in earlier sections, there are always larcenous gas station attendants to contend with, and sticky-fingered hotel staff, and teens looking for an easy score, and the "bad" area of town where the drugs are trafficked and crime is rampant. All of which are easily avoided with a little basic preventative thinking.

The truth is that a life in Mexico will likely prove to be far safer than anything you're accustomed to in the U.S. But again, that won't sell newspapers, and it certainly won't fit any agenda to stem a brain and resource drain out of the U.S., so don't expect to hear about it through any of the established media there.

For now, consider the true state of affairs to be our little secret.

Schools

Most folks with children from outside of Mexico tend to want to have their kids attend private bilingual schools. This is partially because the public schools aren't particularly great, and also because there are plentiful private schools available at moderate cost. In Cabo, for instance, there are around a dozen acclaimed bilingual private schools, with prices ranging from $350 a month for elementary school, to $700 or so per month for high school. Prices are lower in Guadalajara, and far lower in Colima, Merida, etc.

Locating a suitable school is easier with kindergarten

through elementary, and gets more difficult and expensive the higher the grade.

There will generally be an admission fee in addition to the monthly charge, as well as returning student annual enrollment fees (usually equivalent to two month's charge, as it's often used to pay the teachers' two months of paid vacation). The cost of textbooks and other materials is typically pretty reasonable, at least by U.S. standards. Many schools have online websites describing their curriculums and fees, so here again, the Web is a valuable research assistant.

Students with little or no Spanish will find it difficult to assimilate beyond second or third grade, as much of the curriculum will be taught in Spanish, even in the bilingual schools. It's not particularly rare for an American third grader to be entered into second grade in Mexico upon arrival, so his language skills can develop adequately to process the lessons. Fortunately, at a young age, children can pick up languages very quickly. It gets harder as the child ages, so the older your children, the tougher a time they will have coming up to speed. Tutoring can be extremely helpful for the first year, and can be had inexpensively in most areas.

Most students of college age go to one of the larger mainland universities, either in Mexico City, Guadalajara, or Monterrey. And of course, many Gringos and prosperous Mexicans attend American colleges once their high school years are behind them.

In closing, there are plentiful school choices for virtually every age, with private being the preferred alternative.

Child Care

Most areas of Mexico have after-school child care facilities available. Those with children who don't just stay at home with them choose to hire a baby-sitter, due to the extremely low cost of doing so. As an example, a babysitter who will watch a toddler or pre-schooler, and act as a maid for light cleaning, might cost $300 a month for a forty-four-hour week (half day on Saturday) in all areas but Zapopan and Baja, where they might be $50-$100 more. Someone to watch your child after school for four hours a day might cost $110 a month. And that's assuming you're in one of the more expensive areas. If you're in any of my lower cost recommendations, you can probably reduce that by forty percent or more. But don't expect your help to speak any English in that price range, so best to have brushed up on your *Espanol* before moving across the border.

Driving

Driving in Mexico is an adventure not to be taken lightly. Often the locals don't particularly follow any set of rules of the road I've been able to make out, so you have to drive defensively, and be careful at all times. It's not unusual to have a car hurtling the wrong way down a one way, or be going the wrong way along the side of the freeway, if there's a shoulder (not so much in Zapopan or Colima, but definitely in Baja, Chapala, and to a lesser extent, Merida). And in Baja, it's also not unusual to have a cow or goats standing in the middle of the road. In all of Mexico, it's not unheard of for there to be pedestrians crossing a highway, or to come across a bicycle equipped with a popsicle cooler peddling alongside sixty MPH traffic, or to encounter a fifty year old pick-up truck doing twenty mph on the highway in either the fast or slow lane, assuming that the road has more than one lane in each direction. "Expect the unexpected" would be particularly apropos in Mexico.

Always wear your seatbelt. No exceptions.

Speed limits are posted in kilometers, and there are 1.6 kilometers to a mile. So if you're doing eighty KM, that's fifty MPH. Most modern cars have both kilometers and miles marked on their speedometers, so it's fairly straightforward to comply with the rules. Speaking of which, many of the posted speed limits are laughable and are routinely ignored. I leave this to your best judgment, however with the caveat that it's best to be ten minutes late, than dead. The faster you're moving, the less reaction time you have, and reaction time can be everything in avoiding accidents.

Driving at night anywhere but in densely populated areas is hazardous due to cows, goats, and horses on the road. And in Baja, even in densely populated areas, one can encounter the odd cow in the most unexpected areas. This is due to the Mexican custom of allowing livestock to roam free, unrestricted by fences. Basically, cows have the right of way, and if you're unfortunate enough to hit one, not only will it total your front end (at the very least), but you'll be financially responsible to the beast's owner. Night driving is also dangerous because Baja natives like to take the edge off their harsh day with a beer or ten, and then drive. So consider the first paragraph's examples, and then add in the dynamic that many of the drivers will be high or drunk or both. One can quickly see why it's not a great idea to drive at night unless it's a short distance and in town. On mainland the drunk driving laws are more strictly enforced, and as an example, in Zapopan, if you blow over a low threshold, they confiscate your car and jail you. My counsel is if you're going to drink, take Uber or walk.

One driving oddity that has gotten plenty of Gringo tourists T-boned is that on the highway, left turns often must be executed from the far-right, frontage road lane, and not from the left lane. It also causes more than its fair share of rental cars being rear-ended when they stop to make a left from the highway instead of the right lane.

Another oddity is the presence of "*topes*", or speed bumps, on the highway (not on toll roads) and many streets. Often these will be large enough to take your muffler off if you haven't slowed to a crawl, which is the general idea. There may or may not be signs warning you of their presence, and they may or may not be painted yellow, so when driving most streets, again, doing so cautiously is best.

It's a good idea to obey all the traffic signs, however don't expect anyone else to. Stop signs are at best a weak suggestion and at worst a target for spirited beer bottle target practice, so whenever you come to a situation requiring either you or the other guy to stop, just assume he won't. Although at an intersection where nobody has a stop sign the idea is cars alternate from each direction, in reality there's no concept of right of way in Mexico, and you can be easily killed testing that.

Never assume the other guy is even going to be on the correct side of the road, especially in Baja. One young lady I know reported to me that after a late night of tequila drinking, she discovered that at four AM she'd been driving on the wrong side of the highway for five miles before becoming aware of it. Fortunately there was nobody else on the road at that hour, as this particular highway is one of the few that has a center divide island separating the two right lanes from the two left. Point is that would have been a high-speed head-on collision had anyone decided to go fishing before dawn.

It's also not unknown for locals to take shortcuts by going the wrong way on onramps or frontage roads – why drive a mile out of one's way when one can simply go the wrong way for a few hundred yards? This is also frequently done in reverse gear, adding to the challenge of avoiding the oncoming car.

Many older vehicles in Mexico will have mechanical issues, including few functional signal, brake or headlights. That isn't as large a problem as it might seem, as few drivers are inclined to signal anything at any time – I personally believe they think it's a sign of weakness. But coming up on a slow-moving truck with no tail lights at night can prove challenging, especially if you're going fast, and even more so if he's decided to drive in the fast lane. And when it rains, you'll quickly discover that a large percentage of the vehicles on the road don't have functional windshield wipers, creating a whole different set of issues. Many poor driving decisions are predicated on non-functional safety or operating equipment, which makes predicting other drivers' behavior almost impossible.

Tires are also not going to be in particularly good condition on many vehicles, which can result in cars losing traction unexpectedly, as well as in large chunks of shredded tire appearing out of nowhere in the middle of the road.

Often, when moving objects or furniture, the locals will forego the bother of securing the load, and instead trust in God to guide their trip. This results in the sudden appearance of everything from random boxes to couches in the road, as well as cement bags, baby carriages, stray animals, and every imaginable sort of miscellaneous hazard.

My advice is don't drive fast, give other drivers far more room than you normally would, observe signs (especially no passing signs), and be very careful whenever you get behind the wheel. Car accidents are the number one cause of death in Mexico for Gringos. No joke.

Here's a useful list of do's and don'ts when driving in Mexico. It's by no means exhaustive.

- Watch for livestock. Cows, horses, goats. Also watch for dogs, cats, pelicans (yes, pelicans) and buzzards. I actually took a buzzard through my windshield on one of my first trips down Baja (coming around a curve south of Mulege at a fair rate of speed) and the result was basically what you would get if you threw a bowling ball at a windshield at sixty mph. Twenty buzzards went one direction from whatever they were feasting on at the side of the road, and one went the other. I got the stray, and spent three hundred miles holding my windshield together with strapping tape and my hand. Fun drive. Especially in hundred-ten-degree August heat. Point is I could have avoided that by driving slower and being ready with my brakes on first buzzard sighting. I've since developed that habit.

- Be on the lookout for road hazards – potholes a foot deep, rocks the size of footballs, stray junk, bumpers, mufflers, lawn chairs, etc.
- When you see a sign that says *Vado*, it means dip, and you want to slow down for those, as occasionally they can be flooded from mountain runoff. They're also nice spots for livestock to congregate.
- When the car in front of you hits his left turn signal, it usually (although not always) means it's safe to pass. Whether that car is accurate in his assessment is another matter. It can also rarely signal an intent to turn left, however that's a remote likelihood most of the time.
- Don't assume. Anything. Don't assume the other guy's brakes are functional, don't assume he's sober or even sees you, don't assume he'll do anything remotely rational. For that reason, don't ever tailgate. You have literally no idea how the car in front of you will respond, and if he decides you need to be slowed down, you may never see any brake lights.
- Be courteous at all times. You never know when you'll need help, and it could be the guy that you were rude to a few miles back who is your only bet for a long time.
- Maintain your vehicle, especially tires, wipers, brakes and engine oil.
- Expect most drivers to be dead drunk after dark, and on weekends.
- Drive defensively at all times.

Police

There will inevitably come a time where you get pulled over, either by a local cop, or a *Federal,* which is the Mexican equivalent of the Highway Patrol. When that happens, it isn't unusual for the policeman to suggest you can pay your traffic fine on the spot, in order to avoid having to go with him to the station, or have him take your license and have you go to the station to pay the fine and retrieve it. What you do at that point is a moral dilemma, and possibly an opportunity to hone your negotiating skills.

Many will advise you to under no circumstances pay anything on the spot, as it just encourages the cops to attempt to solicit bribes. This is completely true. If you're morally adamant on this point, I'd encourage you to always opt for the "go to the station" option. Reasons are several. First, your fine will probably be 1/5 of whatever the cop is asking. Second, you might be let go because the cop doesn't really want to take an hour out of his money-making time to go with you to the station. Third, it's the ethically correct thing to do.

If you aren't that concerned with cost or ethics, then you should at least negotiate. Best way to do that is to carry a 200 peso note mixed in with a couple of twenty peso notes in whatever pocket you don't normally carry money in, and when it comes time to negotiate, pull out that skimpy wad. The cop will see it and figure he is taking almost all your cash if he settles for 200 pesos. That amounts to about $9 at today's exchange rate. Most cops will start off high, based on what you're driving, how much Spanish you speak, and what you did. For running a stop sign, or doing an illegal U turn (forget the "there's no sign forbidding it" argument, they aren't interested), or speeding, you might be asked for $50 USD for the fine. If you did more, such as passing in a no passing zone and speeding excessively, you might be informed that the fine is $100 USD. It isn't. But many Gringos will pay the "fine" at the asking price, hence the demand. I've found that if you speak reasonable Spanish, and can assure the nice officer that you're both ashamed of your behavior, as well as down on your luck, you can negotiate that down to the 200 peso or so level, using the aforementioned skimpy wad trick.

Note I am not encouraging you to bribe the local police. I'm just saying that some people find that it's the most expedient way to resolve a conflict, and if so, paying more than one has to would be foolish.

Getting Around

Having a vehicle in much of Mexico is an essential. While bus service in the larger areas is good, the plain fact of the matter is you'll need a car, especially if there's an emergency. Taxis are readily available in bigger towns, as are ridesharing services, so that's always an option, however I wouldn't recommend trying to live in Mexico sans car.

On the subject of buses, a lot of the locals use that method of transportation as it's far cheaper than flying. Within the larger metropolitan areas, bus service is very good and services most areas, and cheap – around forty cents U.S. or less. But these will be thirty-year-old school buses with no climate control other than a window that may or may not open, so unless one really insists upon absorbing as much local color as possible, I wouldn't recommend it as everyday transportation. And especially not during flu season, or with a death plague virus spreading like wildfire.

For longer distances, the Mexican inter-city bus system is robust, with everything from first class non-stop buses with movies, food, and drink, to commuter buses that stop at every crossing. They're affordable and leave most cities every few minutes, so are a viable option for most two or three hour hops.

As far as flying goes, Volaris and Viva and Interjet are low cost airlines that offer good service virtually everywhere. I use them all the time, and find them to be efficient and affordable on most of the routes they fly.

Chapter 8

Shipping, Importation and Moving, Pets, Television, Social Networks, Communications, Utilities, Web Resources

Shipping and Mail

Baja

There are a number of companies specializing in shipping items from the U.S. to Baja. They all charge roughly the same prices, and will act as the importer, dealing with customs duties, which currently vary from fifteen percent on up, depending upon what's being imported and where it was manufactured. It's best to check with the shipping companies for the latest tariffs and rules, as they're subject to regular change.

Mainland

I'm not a fan of Mexican customs on shipping anything to mainland, as at least half the time whatever you're importing never arrives, and is held in customs forever. That said, all the usual suspects in international shipping provide reliable service for documents, and DHL, Fed Ex, UPS all have offices in most areas. For domestic shipping, they are all good, as are some of the national companies that specialize in Mexican delivery.

Holders of temp and permanent residence visas get six months to import their household goods with no duties. But anything being imported under this program needs to be used. You can't buy a bunch of new furniture or appliances and ship them down. Customs tends to scrutinize these shipments fairly carefully, and they aren't stupid. You'll need to prepare a list of all items so they can be inventoried, which the shipper will use to interact with Customs as they inspect your shipment, and it'll need to be translated into Spanish so it can be read on the Mexican side of the border.

It really doesn't work out to be particularly cost-effective to buy electronics elsewhere and then import them. Big box retailers like Costco and Sam's Club, as well as WalMart have prices so low on most electronics that there's no real savings buying from the U.S. Ditto for tires, refrigerators, and most appliances.

Mail

The Mexican mail system is primitive by first world standards, and can take forever. Many Gringos living in the Cabo and San Jose Del Cabo areas opt for getting a box at Mailboxes, Etc. or one of its competitors, which have locations in both towns. It's convenient because they have a San Diego location you can have your mail forwarded to, and then they ship it down to Baja.

This doesn't work on mainland, so my advice is don't use the mail for anything you ever want to receive, or have delivered. This isn't an exaggeration. While it's said it's improving, that starts from an extremely low bar, so the best it might do is improve from abysmal to terrible.

Mail forwarding via the postal system in Mexico won't work, as it requires additional postage to mail in Mexico. I would advise anyone moving here to go electronic with all of your U.S. bills and credit cards, as that way you can check their status and pay them online. Paper mail is really a thing of the past these days, as virtually all goods and services have online presences.

Alternatively, you can have a trusted friend collect your mail, and DHL it to you once a month, however that can run $35 or more per shipment (depending upon weight) and none of it will be current.

Moving

Most folks moving from the U.S. use one of the many freight companies dedicated to getting your stuff from the U.S. to wherever you're going to live in Mexico. Costs are generally similar, as the cost of importation, gas, and labor doesn't really change much from company to company. A list of moving and shipping companies follows in the Web Resources section.

My advice is to leave as much of your old life back home as possible. As discussed before, a fair amount of the rental market comes furnished, and furniture is relatively inexpensive if you buy or build a place, so shipping a bunch of used furniture to Mexico doesn't make much sense unless you're in love with it. Silverware and utensils are an exception. But the reality is that you aren't going to need much of what you have up north – your wardrobe will be primarily warm-weather/tropical gear, and with the exception of computers, medicine, and personal effects, the cost of hauling it down is usually higher than the cost of simply buying new as you require things.

Many expats in my area buy their furniture from Guadalajara, and the craftsmanship is beautiful and relatively cheap. Unless you're absolutely married to that seven-year-old Lazy Boy or Grandma's dining room table, you'll find it's a better deal to just buy locally. There are exceptions, and if you're willing to spend many hours acquiring other people's used furniture on Craigslist or a similar platform, the combination of cost and tariffs and shipping can make sense. But if you compare apples to apples, buying locally generally is a better way to go.

When it comes to choosing a shipper you should ask around, as well as consult the various message boards. There are more than a few who do an excellent job, but have no website, so often word of mouth is their only form of advertising. For example, I use a group in Cabo which has reliably transported items for me for years, and which has no idea that something like the Internet even exists. They understand trucks, and loading and packing, not technology, so if you want their contact info, don't look online, as you won't find it.

The local phone book would be the final place I would look, but with a highly skeptical eye, as you have no idea how reliable a company you find in the phone book is. Again, I'd put the name out there on the message boards to see what kind of feedback you get before hiring anyone to handle your prized possessions. You'll also want to ensure they are bonded and have insurance, because sometimes things get broken or lost, and if you're dealing with an outfit that has two guys and a truck, your likelihood of recourse is low.

Here is a good website that details the ins and outs more thoroughly: https://www.thespruce.com/moving-household-items-overseas-to-mexico-2436075

Weather Tracking

Baja

Baja's storm season is short, but decisive. From August through mid-October, hurricanes and tropical storms are a danger, and about once or twice per season one will hit some area of southern or central Baja. There are a number of online resources available for tracking storms and getting up-to-the-minute information. Some of my favorites are listed below:

First is the U.S. National Weather Service site.

www.nhc.noaa.gov/text/refresh/MIATWOEP+shtml/301826.shtml

Others include BajaInsider.com's service, and EEBMike.com's hurricane tracking page.

www.bajainsider.com/weather/easternpacifichurricanes208.htm

http://www.eebmike.com/

The damage caused by hurricanes in Baja is very real, and they can cause massive flooding, disruption of power and phone service, road closures, and the complete halt of any goods coming down the peninsula (in the case of road washouts, which are not infrequent).

I'd suggest you store at least a week's supply of drinking water and canned/packaged food (nothing requiring refrigeration), flashlights, batteries, candles, matches, and any medications wherever you're staying. Many homes in Baja take the additional step of having a backup generator in the event power goes out – I'd recommend having one if at all possible, with propane being the best bet for fuel (gasoline generators are dangerous, as they tend to get hot and explode at the most inopportune times, i.e. while you're refueling them), whereas propane generators are permanently hooked into a home's propane line, requiring no hazardous handling.

I'd also recommend getting your propane tank filled to the brim during storm season, and keeping it topped off every month so you always have a full tank in August, September and October. That will ensure you can cook and will have hot water, even if power is out for several days.

Aside from hurricane shutters (either fabric or metal) natives will often put plywood over larger glass surfaces. And to my annual amazement, you'll see locals dutifully affixing tape in large X shapes on all their glass, which shows a complete lack of understanding of basic physics. If a wind is high enough to break glass, say a hundred and fifty plus mph, it will also be powerful enough to break tape. I suppose the theory is that the tape will hold the pieces of the window together if it breaks, but just imagine a window mounted on the wing of a plane on takeoff, and then imagine tape (and adhesive) strong enough to hold it together if it breaks. Pretty simple to see the conceptual problem with the tape paradigm, but that doesn't stop anyone. My advice is skip that step, as it inevitably just bakes the adhesive onto the glass, which you can never completely get off, and achieves nothing of value.

Mainland

I use Windy.com to forecast everything from wind to temps to rain in all the other areas I've mentioned. I've found no more accurate resource, and highly recommend it. https://www.windy.com/

Pets

Bringing pets to Mexico is straightforward whether you're driving or flying. If you plan to fly your pet down, you'll need to check with the specific airline in order to confirm the exact requirements, which can differ among airlines, and get the paperwork listed below. If you're driving, there's not much to do other than to obtain the two requisite documents you'll need and one crate per pet, whether they travel by air or car:

1. A vaccination certificate stating your pet has been vaccinated against rabies (required annually in MX), hepatitis, pip and leptospirosis.

2. An official health certificate that must be issued by a veterinarian no more than 72 hours before entering Mexico.

There's a limitation of two large pets (cats or dogs) for importation. If you plan to bring more, you'll need to get written permission from the nearest Mexican Consulate before your trip.

Many expats have pets, and they seem to adjust readily to the warmer environment. One thing to note is that tick and flea-borne diseases are more worrisome in Mexico, so it's essential you use Frontline or similar product with regularity, and also give your animals frequent baths with flea and tick shampoo. You'll also want to give your pet anti-heartworm medication to avoid that infestation. Most of the diseases in Mexico are easily treatable if caught in the early stages. There are now 5-in-1 tests that will screen for the most common ailments, and I get my dogs tested annually. It's just good preventative medicine, and avoids future heartache.

Distemper is common in Mexico, as is Erlichia, a tick-borne illness that can be terminal if not treated in time. Mange is a frequent scourge of street dogs, Parvo kills many puppies each year, and a host of parasitical infections await dogs allowed to roam free, which most natives seem to feel is the natural order of things. I keep my dogs in the house or in my dog run, and have had no problems with any of the above – but that's because I'm extremely cautious of any environment where other dogs have been.

If you don't own a pet but are considering one, there are

many deserving cats and dogs at the Humane Society shelters in Mexico. I've had at least ten Mexican rescue dogs, either fosters or beloved permanent pets, and can say without equivocation they are the best dogs I've ever owned. It's like they know you saved them from shelter hell, and they never forget to appreciate you the more for it. They quickly adapt to English commands, so there's no insurmountable language barrier. If you want unconditional love, a rescue is the way to go.

Television

Mexico really only has one broadcast option for English speakers: Satellite TV. While many areas now have cable, English content can vary from nil to marginal.

The primary provider is Sky TV. Info can be obtained by going to their website at:
http://www.sky.com.mx/

You can also bring your own satellite dish down and have a tech hook it up, if you want to keep your U.S. service.

That said, I get Netflix and Amazon Prime, and all streaming options that are available in the US seem to be available in Mexico as well. So I don't even bother with satellite, as the Internet has made it a moot point.

Social Networks

Expats in Mexico have a plethora of options in terms of

social networks. Primary among these are Internet-based message boards, where Gringos communicate with each other on a wide variety of topics. All you have to do is perform a search with your town or region name, and they'll pop up. There are also typically plentiful in-person gatherings in expat-dense areas like Cabo, Guadalajara, Chapala, and Merida. The lesser known spots, like Zapopan and Colima, will obviously have fewer groups, so most would be advised to stick to the internet in those areas.

Larger metro areas also feature every sort of network, from charities to social clubs (like Cabo Tomatoes for women) to AA to exercise-groups to church-based organizations. They are too numerous to mention, and constantly evolving, so it isn't practical to attempt to list them in this book.

Social networks can provide a valuable framework for companionship, sharing tips, and avoiding feelings of isolation that can occur when relocating to a foreign land. Man is a social animal, and participation in one or two groups can make the move far easier, as hearing the experiences of others who've lived in the area for years will prove invaluable in understanding the culture and in acclimating to your surroundings.

Communication (Cell and Phone, Internet)

Every area of Mexico now has modern internet and cell coverage.

Cell service is available from Telcel and Movistar and Nextel. A number of different plans are available, and it's best to consult with the various providers for their latest offerings. One that gets a lot of use is the Telcel "Amigo Plan" offering, whereby you can purchase cards preloaded with minutes, and then for a nominal one-time activation fee have a Baja number, using the cards for air time. That's probably the most painless as an initial possibility, as you can use it for a few months, see how much calling you actually do, and then compare the cost via Amigo versus a full-time plan. One note is that all cell numbers have to be registered with the Mexican government to cut down on crime, so your ID will be required to get a number.

Land-line telephone service is provided by Telmex. Telmex has offices in most metro areas, and several of the smaller towns. In order to get Telmex service you'll typically have to provide a utility bill and ID, and then have to wait for indeterminate timeframes to actually have service activated. This is one area you'll need to work on your patience, as the phone company can often promise to have service up in a week, and three weeks later still have failed to come out and hook you up. It's a typically large, inefficient bureaucracy, made far worse by the fact that it has a monopoly within the country, so there is no choice B. Waiting in line can easily take an hour or longer, so don't plan much on the days you visit Telmex.

Telmex also provides Internet services via their Infinitum product offerings, which deliver various speeds of service at different price points. Go to the Telmex website in order to see the latest plans, as they change regularly. www.Telmex.com/mx

Megacable also now offers good, reliable internet service in most of Mexico. I've used both Telmex and Megacable and they both provide the same experience, which includes indifferent customer service and annoying installation times, but since there are no other options in most places, that's what you get.

In Zapopan, because it's a larger market, you also have Totalplay and Izzi. You can find them online. I have no idea how good or bad they are, however it would be pretty difficult to not be able to do better than Megacable and Telmex on bedside manner…

Voice-over-IP services work all over Mexico. Additionally, Internet calling by services like Skype allow you to speak with others over the Internet at no cost, as do Zoom, Google Talk, and a handful of others. The Internet services have transformed the cost of calling internationally from a significant issue to a non-issue, and most of the folks I know use the Internet for all their long-distance communications.

Utilities (propane, electricity)

Electricity is provided by CFE, the national power company. This group is another monopoly, and thus their service tends to be typically bureaucratic. In order to secure power for your rental or home, you'll need to go to the CFE office and provide a variety of identification papers, along with proof of residence (like a rental contract or your Fideicomiso or property deed). Activation can take several days, so it's best to do this in advance of moving in and taking possession. This is another place where lines can be long, so bring a book and plenty of patience.

Electricity is more expensive than in the U.S., so practicing energy saving techniques like only operating lights and AC in whatever room you are in become mandatory lest you wind up with massive energy bills. I have solar, and use it to power my home, and send any overage back to CFE, so my power bill each month comes to $5 when my neighbors are paying hundreds of dollars per month during peak heat season in Cabo. In Merida, it's an absolute must if you want to avoid thousands, or even five figures, in electricity bills over a year. I highly recommend solar if you buy or build a home as the cost of panels has dropped to next to nothing, and a full house system can be had for the cost of 4 or 5 years of energy bills you'll never have to pay again.

Water in Baja comes from OOMSAPAS, and you'll need to activate service in much the same way as with CFE, unless your landlord includes it as part of the rent.

On mainland, each municipality has its own water provider, which any realtor can explain to you in seconds. One note on water in Mexico – in the U.S., water pressure is delivered from the city via your water pipes. In Mexico, each home is equipped with an electric water pump, and a cistern which the city water fills, acting as a reservoir. It's very much like a boat or an RV with a water reservoir, and a pump to get it from the reservoir to your tap. Thus, if power goes out, unless you have a gravity fed water system where the cistern is on the roof (typically only in the most inexpensive homes), your water pump won't operate, and you'll be out of luck on water until the power goes back on.

Gas is provided by a number of gas companies, and delivered to your home with a phone call via truck. Unlike in the U.S., propane/LP gas comes in canisters or a propane truck, and storage is at your home in a tank or cylinder. Water heaters, stoves, and dryers typically operate on propane in Mexico, which is not centrally delivered via a pipe like in the U.S. It's important to know where your propane tank is, and to check it periodically to see how full it is (it has a meter on it showing fill level). When it runs to around 15%, you'll want to phone your neighborhood gas company and have a truck come out and refill it. Payment is on the spot, in cash only. A word of warning: if you have a pool or Jacuzzi and plan to heat it, you'll find that a pool or spa heater can deplete hundreds of dollars of gas in a matter of a few days. It becomes even more critical to regularly monitor your propane levels if you plan to heat your pool or spa, or you can run out of gas in startling time, and possibly be waiting days for a truck to come refill you.

Water and power have a zero tolerance for late payments, which has arisen from the locals' often chronic procrastination, which naturally extends to paying for anything. So it's very important to pay your utilities on time, or they will shut it off the day after the due date. Resumption of service typically involves a fee, as well as a wait to get re-initiated which can involve days, so it's best to stay on top of this. Fortunately, both CFE and water can be paid online, so you can handle this without waiting in lines. Alternatively, you can hire a property manager, which isn't a bad idea if you're only going to live in Mexico part time, as you don't want to discover a burst pipe or termites eating their way through your carpentry after months of ongoing damage.

Web Resources

Facebook has a number of good expat groups you can find by searching for "expat" and whatever city or country you want.

Here are a few Websites for general information on Mexico:

http://www.rollybrook.com/how_to_move_to_mexico.htm

http://www.soniadiaz.mx/

http://www.mexconnect.com/

http://www.loscabosguide.com/

http://www.mexperience.com/liveandwork/living_in_mexic
o.htm

http://www.bajawesternonion.com/

http://bajainsider.com/

http://www.bajaquest.com/bajalinks/

Message boards for information sharing, classifieds, rentals, etc.:

Baja:
http://forums.mexonline.com/index.php

http://bajaforums.com/

http://forums.bajanomad.com/

http://www.talkbaja.com/

Mainland:

https://www.expatforum.com/expats/mexico-expat-forum-expats-living-mexico/

https://www.expatsinmexico.com/

https://yucatanexpatlife.com/

https://www.expatexchange.com/

Shipping and Moving companies:

http://www.acv.com.mx/

http://www.columbiaexport.com/

http://www.bajafreight.com/

http://www.castores.com.mx/

Apartment and Real Estate Hunting:

http://www.Inmuebles24.com

http://www.Trovit.com.mx

Preparation for Moving

The day comes you've decided you want to make the move, but you aren't sure how to prepare or keep everything organized. The following punch list is organized around specific preparations you should make, beginning a few months before you move. Obviously, depending upon your situation, you'll need to focus on different aspects. For instance, if you're married with children, your prep will be substantially different than if you're single. This list assumes you'll be driving across the border. Obviously, if flying, you'll need to book flights and confirm airline policy regarding pets (if appropriate).

60 Days Out

1) **Passports and other ID.** Make sure your passport is valid and doesn't expire for at least a year. It will make your visa application much easier, as otherwise you'll have to renew it, and then start the visa process over again. If you have children or a mate, they'll need passports too. You can keep your driver's license, so just also make sure that doesn't expire for at least a year as well.
2) **Visas.** Apply for your visa(s) at the Mexican Consulate, if you're going to stay in Mexico for more than 180 days. Same applies if you intend to work or get an investor visa.
3) **Pets.** If you plan to take pets to Mexico, make sure their vaccinations are all current, and plan with your vet to get a health certificate no more than 72 hours before you cross the border. Contact your Mexican Consulate and confirm the process for bringing your pet(s) into the country.
4) **Vehicles and Real Estate.** Figure out what you want

to do with any vehicle(s) not going with you to Mexico. Place ads to sell any car you don't plan to take or store or leave with someone trusted. If you plan to make your move permanent, you should already have your U.S. home listed with a broker and on the market. If renting, plan to give notice soon.

5) **Housing.** If you plan to stay in a hotel for a bit while you scope out neighborhoods in Mexico, book your reservations. If you've already found a rental, you should have inked a deal to move in.

6) **Possessions**. Make a list of everything you have, and decide what you plan to take or ship, and what will be left permanently behind. Start having garage sales, or otherwise dispose of anything you plan to get rid of.

7) **Moving Company.** Get competitive bids from several companies to move your stuff. Get recent references, and call them. Once you feel comfortable with a company, engage them to handle the move. Make a list of everything you plan to take, along with the estimated used value of each item, and have it translated into Spanish.

8) **Schools.** Contact several target schools and arrange for interviews when you first arrive.

9) **Mail.** Communicate with your list of contacts and arrange for a change of address. If you're going to rent a home, use that address. If Mailboxes, etc., use that. Convert all your credit card and routine bills to electronic format and let the companies know not to mail paper statements.

10) **Financial and Taxes.** Organize your proof of income – either pension statements, payroll or bank statements. Plan to carry all important paperwork with you, i.e. bonds, stock certs, etc. Talk to a CPA or other tax planning professional and clarify your tax position and strategy moving forward.

30 Days Out

1) **Passports and Visas**. You should have all of these attended to by now. If you're missing any, prioritize securing them.

2) **Belongings.** You should be actively selling, donating, giving away or disposing of all belongings you don't plan to take with you.

3) **Medical Records & Prescriptions.** Get copies of all medical records and prescriptions. If you have any exotic medications, arrange with your doctor to get long term supplies of them, and resign yourself to coming back home periodically to resupply. Once you're in Mexico, you'll need to check with the pharmacies in your target area and confirm they carry or will order the meds. You can also try Farmacias Guadalajara online.

4) **Home.** If renting, give notice (if you haven't already done so). If selling, hopefully you're closing by now, and can have your realtor handle it. If still on the market, formulate a plan for dealing with a close remotely.

5) **Mail.** Contact all relevant vendors and service providers and inform them of your move. This includes phone company, cell provider, utilities, TV, banks, gyms, schools, etc.

6) **Banking**. Arrange to close any bank accounts you don't plan to keep active while in Mexico.

7) **Pets**. Write a reminder to get your pet(s) health certificate from your veterinarian no more than 3 days before you leave.

8) **Automobiles**. Get the oil and transmission fluid in your Baja car changed (filters too) and check spare and regular tire condition if you're planning to bring one to Baja – if anything looks iffy, replace it. Assemble a roadside emergency kit. Get your brakes checked, belts inspected, and

all fluids topped off, including radiator fluid. Verify the registration's valid for at least 6 months. Plan on taking the pink slip for importation, assuming it qualifies.

D-Day

1) **Automobile.** Get Mexican auto insurance before you cross the border if you haven't already. Gas up just before the border.

2) **Packing.** If you haven't already packed, it's time to do so. Keep all medications where you can easily reach them; same for important papers and travel documents.

3) **Home.** Your fridge and freezer should be empty. All trash should be gone, or put outside for removal. Collect keys and garage door openers and have them ready to return to landlord or realtor.

4) **Money.** Make sure you have adequate cash to carry you for several weeks to a month. Just assume when you cross the border your credit cards or ATM may not work in some towns. For whatever reason.

5) **Meters.** Get final meter readings for all utilities. You should have arranged to pay these online, so this is just for your reference.

6) **Walkthrough.** Do a final walkthrough to make sure you got everything. There's nothing worse than having forgotten something and realizing it a thousand miles from home. Ideally, do so with your landlord so you can hand him the keys at the end of it.

Sample Budget

The following is a sample monthly budget. Obviously, you can add items or adjust amounts to suit your situation and requirements. I'd suggest you create one before moving to Mexico, and then go through it after a few months and see how realistic it is. Remember electricity is more expensive than in the U.S., and everything else is less expensive, with the exception of a few marquis areas. This also assumes you eat out multiple times per week, have a maid once a week, pay a gardener, use a fair amount of AC 6 months a year, are accruing auto maintenance dollars monthly, and do the same for doctor and dentist visits, and drive a couple hundred miles per week.

Utilities	$200.00
Rent	$500.00
Maid (twice weekly)	$100.00
Gardener	$100.00
Food	$500.00
Gas	$100.00
Car Insurance & Registration	$80.00
Health & Other Insurance	$150.00
Medicine	$50.00
Auto Maintenance	$50.00
Entertainment	$100.00
Phone, TV	$100.00
Healthcare	$50.00
Emergency Contingency	$100.00
Total	$2180.00

Chapter 9

–

Living The Dream

You've been in your chosen Mexican area for about two months now, and find yourself settling in. Let's assume you did as I did, and chose the Cabo or San Jose del Cabo area to call your home.

Your day starts at around eight, with some juice and a snack bar. You then meet up with friends to do an hour hike in the hills, before it gets hot out. You discuss the latest restaurants everyone has tried, as well as some current events. Everyone you encounter on the trail says "*Hola*" to you, as do you. Your group is a quirky, ever-changing bunch, with both men and women, all Gringos. A few bring their dogs along. Some days nobody shows up, some days 4 people. It's unpredictable.

Back at home, you shower, and then go down to the beach for a late breakfast with a new friend who is considering opening a business in town. A few hours pass as you consider his options, as well as the great food and scenery. The waves make a pleasant noise as they wash up onto the beach, and you can faintly hear the drone of a sport-fishing boat trolling offshore.

Next up is running some errands. Going to WalMart to get some aspirin, Costco or City Club to pick up your favorite soda and some tequila and limes for cocktail hour tonight at your house, which has become a ritual, often with guests joining you to enjoy the sunset. You go to the fresh produce market and select a basket of vegetables, but time's gotten away from you (again) and you realize you're going to run late (again) if you aren't careful.

You remember you have a round of golf planned at two with some other new friends over at one of the big courses in San Jose. You've decided you'll grab lunch on the way, either fresh fish tacos or sizzling steak tacos at your favorite grill – it's always a tough call, as both are cheap and very tasty. As you chomp away, you chat with some tourists who just "discovered" your favorite quick food stop, and enjoy the look of amazement and envy on their faces when everyone does the obligatory, "Where are you from?" and you tell them you live here.

After golf, you just make it home in time for a late siesta, which lasts an hour or so. Refreshed, you don your evening formal wear – a Hawaiian shirt and shorts, with flip flops – and start squeezing limes for cocktail hour. Your neighbors come over at seven, with some friends who arrived this afternoon from back home, and everyone socializes until the sun sets.

Everyone has decided dinner tonight will be Argentine steak, with gourmet Italian losing out by a slim margin. So off you go, stopping by the local wine shop to pick up a Malbec you've been meaning to try. The restaurant is semi-outdoor, so there's a fresh breeze off the ocean keeping things comfortable. Dinner winds up taking three hours, between all the conversation, appetizers, main course, desert, and more wine and a nightcap.

You debate the idea of taking the newly arrived folks out to some of the nightspots, of which there are too many to mention. Opting for a relatively early evening you bow out, as you've tentatively agreed to go fishing with another new acquaintance tomorrow at six-thirty, and want to get at least six or seven hours of shut-eye.

Sound incredible? That's the day most expats who've retired to the area have, with regularity.

The only difference you may experience is you're the one who has friends visiting regularly, or your kids. Perhaps you go surfing every morning for a few hours instead of hiking. Or maybe you sleep in, preferring to enjoy the freedom to wake up whenever you feel like it. The point is that every day is like your best vacation ever, and it just keeps going on and on. Maybe golf isn't your game, and you prefer cruising the Web for a few hours, or going to one of the large malls in town to see what's new.

Mexico has a way of working its way into your soul, and it can take a while for you to lose the Gringo impatience and anxiety that are constants back home, but you will. Trust me, everyone eventually does.

One of the best things about living here, besides the amazing weather and the awe-inspiring natural beauty, is the palpable sense of relaxation and ease that is the norm. Sure, you can go hit the nightlife and carry on till the early hours of the morning, but most of the time you'll find yourself slipping more into a calmer, more tranquil existence where friendship and family and meals are the central attractions, as opposed to keeping up with the Joneses.

There's something in the water that demands a different pace, one that seems healthier and more in touch with your internal rhythm. There's often nothing you have planned that can't wait until tomorrow. Similarly, there isn't anything scheduled for tomorrow that absolutely has to get done. So you find yourself instead floating along on a Mexican current of life that has your blood pressure twenty points lower than it was a year ago, and your peace of mind double.

I've been asked whether I miss anything about "The Old Country" up north, and I have to say, truthfully, no. I feel like my quality of life is vastly superior to anything I ever experienced when I lived there, and my expenses are half what they were. I find I prioritize different things than I used to, and I have far more friends and acquaintances than I did back home. I like that I know several people whenever I go to the bank or the market, and that my favorite restaurants all know me by name and remember my favorite dishes.

I'm not trying to over-romanticize Mexico, however I think it's hard to do so. The place really is one of those seductive, romantic destinations, one of the magical places under the sun, like Hawaii was decades ago before much of it turned into a tourist machine.

Mexico still has a rough-around-the-edges charm for me that no other place has, and I truly feel like the last five years went by in a heartbeat, while at the same time, took forever due to the pace. I don't go on vacation anywhere any more, because I live where I used to go when I could leave for vacation. And it's never gotten old for me.

So far, so good.

When you get done reading about it and have visited a few times to see what all the fuss is about, I'm convinced that you too will decide there's no better place to be. And then I'll see you around the local watering hole, or down by the docks when the fish come in, or at one or my restaurants. Just wave, and I'll likely wave back. We're mostly friendly like that down Mexico way.

So what are you waiting for?

About the Author

Featured in *The Wall Street Journal, The Times,* and *The Chicago Tribune,* Russell Blake is *The NY Times* and *USA Today* bestselling author of over fifty novels.

Blake is co-author of *The Eye of Heaven* and *The Solomon Curse,* with legendary author Clive Cussler. Blake's novel *King of Swords* has been translated into German, *The Voynich Cypher* into Bulgarian, and his JET novels into Spanish, German, and Czech.

Non-fiction includes the international bestseller *An Angel With Fur* (animal biography), *How To Sell A Gazillion eBooks In No Time* (even if drunk, high or incarcerated), a parody of all things writing-related, and *Retirement Secrets of Mexico.*

Blake writes under the moniker R.E. Blake in the NA/YA/Contemporary Romance genres. Novels include *Less Than Nothing, More Than Anything,* and *Best Of Everything.*

Having resided in Mexico for a dozen years, Blake enjoys his dogs, fishing, boating, tequila and writing, while battling world domination by clowns. His thoughts, such as they are, can be found at his blog: RussellBlake.com

Visit RussellBlake.com for updates

or subscribe to: RussellBlake.com/contact/mailing-list

Books by Russell Blake

Thrillers

FATAL EXCHANGE
FATAL DECEPTION
THE GERONIMO BREACH
ZERO SUM
THE DELPHI CHRONICLE TRILOGY
THE VOYNICH CYPHER
SILVER JUSTICE
UPON A PALE HORSE
DEADLY CALM
RAMSEY'S GOLD
EMERALD BUDDHA
THE GODDESS LEGACY
A GIRL APART
A GIRL BETRAYED
QUANTUM SYNAPSE

The Assassin Series

KING OF SWORDS
NIGHT OF THE ASSASSIN
RETURN OF THE ASSASSIN
REVENGE OF THE ASSASSIN
BLOOD OF THE ASSASSIN
REQUIEM FOR THE ASSASSIN
RAGE OF THE ASSASSIN

The Day After Never Series

THE DAY AFTER NEVER – BLOOD HONOR
THE DAY AFTER NEVER – PURGATORY ROAD
THE DAY AFTER NEVER – COVENANT
THE DAY AFTER NEVER – RETRIBUTION
THE DAY AFTER NEVER – INSURRECTION
THE DAY AFTER NEVER – PERDITION
THE DAY AFTER NEVER – HAVOC
THE DAY AFTER NEVER – LEGION
THE DAY AFTER NEVER – NEMESIS
THE DAY AFTER NEVER – RUBICON

Books by Russell Blake

Co-authored with Clive Cussler
THE EYE OF HEAVEN
THE SOLOMON CURSE

The JET Series
JET
JET II – BETRAYAL
JET III – VENGEANCE
JET IV – RECKONING
JET V – LEGACY
JET VI – JUSTICE
JET VII – SANCTUARY
JET VIII – SURVIVAL
JET IX – ESCAPE
JET X – INCARCERATION
JET XI – FORSAKEN
JET XII – ROGUE STATE
JET XIII – RENEGADE
JET XIV – DARK WEB
JET XV – SAHARA
JET – OPS FILES (prequel)
JET – OPS FILES; TERROR ALERT

The BLACK Series
BLACK
BLACK IS BACK
BLACK IS THE NEW BLACK
BLACK TO REALITY
BLACK IN THE BOX

Non Fiction
AN ANGEL WITH FUR
HOW TO SELL A GAZILLION EBOOKS
(while drunk, high or incarcerated)
RETIREMENT SECRETS OF MEXICO

Made in the USA
Las Vegas, NV
11 November 2024